T0137580

Eternal Security:
Is it Biblical?

How Many Sins Must I Sin to Lose My Salvation?

DR. PHIL BERRY

Order this book online at www.trafford.com
or email orders@trafford.com

Most Trafford titles are also available at major online book retailers.

Printed in the United States of America.

ISBN: 978-1-4269-1965-7 (sc)
ISBN: 978-1-4269-1966-4 (hc)

Library of Congress Control Number: 2009940717

Trafford rev. 11/24/2010

 www.trafford.com

North America & International
toll-free: 1 888 232 4444 (USA & Canada)
phone: 250 383 6864 ♦ fax: 812 355 4082

Dedication

First and foremost I would like to thank the Lord Jesus Christ for allowing me to complete this project which is so dear to my heart, and to my wife Rita who has been so patient with me as I have labored with this project.There have been a lot of early-morning writing and even more late-night studying and research.

I would also like dedicate this book to my uncle Denver who was anticipating being able to read this book, but has since passed away before it was completed.

A special thank you to the guy I consider to be my pastor and good friend Dr.Shawn Wasson. Pastor Thank you for your words of encouragement.

Last but not least I would like to thank Bro. Bill Jetton. Thank you so much for reading the book and giving me your input.

Biography

Philip Berry has been pastor, teacher in Baptist churches in the Chicago area and in southeast Missouri for over 25 years. Pastor Berry started his ministry in the streets of Chicago where he was involved in inner-city ministries, which included ministering to gang bangers, street preaching, and preaching at Pacific Garden Mission. After his call to ministry Pastor Berry thought it was important to be educated, so he began his education at Liberty Bible Institute and continued his studies at Covington Theological Seminary where he earned his undergraduate degrees, from there he attended Masters graduate school of Divinity where he earned his doctorate degree.

How shall we escape The Judgment of God?

Table of Contents

Introduction

Most people I know make no bones as to where they stand on certain issues of life, such as which political party they belong to, their philosophies on religion, and a whole host of other things, but when it comes to the doctrine of eternal security many people want to be on the fence. We live in a politically correct society today and nobody wants to hurt anybody else's feelings. One thing that is certain you will not find any political correctness in the words of Jesus. The children of God should be no different. Whatever the Word of God says is what we should teach and preach and also what we should believe.

In my recent study and research for this project I have come to the conclusion that there are many books written on the subject of eternal security. Most that I have come across have been on the negative side and written against eternal security. Don't get me wrong. There are many good books on the subject of eternal security such as Charles Stanley "Eternal Security" and there is a book out by Charles Ryrie "So Great Salvation", "Arthur Pink on Eternal Security". I know that there are perhaps other note worthy books that I have failed to mention only for a plain and simple fact that I have not read them.

I would like to argue the point that there is a legitimate reason for conforming to the doctrine of eternal security. The study of biblical doctrines has been a life long learning and in turn teaching experience for me it is a big part of my ministry. We will be looking at several other doctrines along the way that I believe will enhance our study on this most crucial doctrine of eternal security. I have always thought that this doctrine was from God. Now through careful research and in-depth study I have concluded that this doctrine can only be of God.

I have studied and taught on these subjects many times. Yet I still come away with a sense that people just do not believe that they can be saved forever. I believe that the doctrine of eternal security plays a very important part in our lives when it comes to salvation. If we can't believe that God can keep us saved, how do we know for sure that He can save us at all? I am very hopeful that through the scriptures and careful research on this subject, I will be able to help those who read this book to be more open minded about the subject and perhaps even change their mind about it. Most people want to throw the "me" syndrome on God, as if it is up to us to keep our salvation. We had nothing to do with salvation to start with how in the world are we going to have anything to do with keeping it after we have received it?

I believe that God wants his children to truly know that there is absolutely nothing that can separate us from His love. May God richly bless those who read this book and for those of you who do not believe in eternal security, it is my prayer that you will read the book with an open mind and then draw your own conclusion.

Romans 8:35-39

[35] *Who shall separate us from the love of Christ? Shall tribulation, or distress, or persecution, or famine, or nakedness, or peril, or sword?* [36] *As it is written, For thy sake we are killed*

all the day long; we are accounted as sheep for the slaughter. [37] *Nay, in all these things we are more than conquerors through him that loved us.* [38] *For I am persuaded, that neither death, nor life, nor angels, nor principalities, nor powers, nor things present, nor things to come,* [39] *Nor height, nor depth, nor any other creature, shall be able to separate us from the love of God, which is in Christ Jesus our Lord.*

Chapter 1

Learning to Study the Bible for Yourself

Before we get to the subject at hand I think we should approach it from an analytical standpoint. We should try to focus our attention on the reasoning behind eternal security. What are some of the reasons why I should trust this doctrine? Is this a man-made doctrine as some suppose that it is, or is it a denominational thing as some would have you to believe, or is it straight from God? Why is this a hot topic among Christian groups? Why is this doctrine so controversial?

There are several topics that need to be addressed in this book, which I believe go right along side the doctrine of eternal security. These are all basic doctrines that for some reason or another we have failed to teach in our churches and perhaps even in our seminaries. I believe that if you conducted a survey of people, asking if they believed that the Bible is the Word of God, most would say they did. Even if you talk to Christians and asked them if they believe that the Bible is God's word most would say they did. But believing it is the Word of God and actually living it are two different things. That is where we have failed as leaders in our churches because we have neglected to teach our parishioners or church members, however you prefer it, these crucial doctrines of the Bible. Is it at all possible that if you don't believe in the doctrine of eternal security then you cannot have the true assurance of salvation?

I think that as in any worthwhile study, it is well worth the effort to start at the beginning (basic truths). I wish I could give you a percentage of how many Christians actually study and understand the Bible. I am sure that the percentage would be low therefore I would like to start this book by talking about the importance of personal Bible study. I really believe one of the reasons why our churches are so weak is that the so-called Christians in our churches never spend any personal time in Bible study. Most people depend upon the pastor to spend good quality time in sermon preparation so that he can deliver a good 20 minute sermon and that is the extent of their Bible study. There are some Christians out there that have been saved for 10, 20, 30 years and do not know how to find certain passages in the Bible and don't know how to do a personal Bible study or even find answers to difficult questions in the Bible. I consider this a sin on the church leaders. Most of the time we want people to walk the aisle to get them to say the "sinners prayer" and that is as far as we take it, our churches really need to incorporate disciple making classes, in depth Bible study and scripture memorization.

Sometimes I have to wonder if we really believe the Bible is the Word of God because if we really believed it would we not spend more time reading it, studying it, meditating on it and praying over the Scriptures? You may be thinking, "Well I can read the Bible okay but I just don't understand it." Listen, if you are a born again Christian, God has given you the spirit of understanding His word. It doesn't come naturally, but by allowing the Holy Spirit of God to open our spiritual eyes and ears so that we can listen to the Word of God, with hard work, we can diligently seek the truth of God's Word and God's Word is truth. The natural man or "the unsaved man" cannot understand the Word of God he may try his best to read it and study it but he will never get the truths of God's Word. That is because the Holy Spirit is not living within him to give him discernment of spiritual things.

In this section I would like to give you some methods for studying God's Word and answering some difficult questions. Some might be thinking even right now, "How do I know that the Bible is God's Word? It seems to contradict itself." Most of the time when people think that the Bible contradicts itself it is because they have no idea their selves of what the Bible really says on certain issues or topics. Those who think that the Bible contradicts itself might take one verse and then look at another verse that doesn't exactly match what they wanted to say. They take the Word of God out of context and say, "See I told you the Bible is full of contradictions."

Once again let me reiterate, the natural man's eyes are blinded to the things of God. I would like to settle this discussion once and for all. Christians really need a way to defend themselves from spiritual warfare the Bible says in I Peter 5:8 - Be sober, be vigilant; because your adversary the devil, as a roaring lion, walketh about, seeking whom he may devour:

Without proper knowledge of the Bible, Christians are weak and feeble and will be chewed up and spit out by the adversary. Whether we are studying doctrines or passages of Scripture or just reading the Scriptures there are several things that we must take into account. The first thing we must get settled is who can study the Word of God?

In order for one to understand the Word of God it is essential that one has to be a Christian that is to say born-again, regenerated. He must be a believer in the Lord Jesus Christ. Any questions so far? If you are not a born again Christian you cannot understand the Word of God.

First of all, and this is very basic we must start studying the Word of God by reading it. We must read it before we can study it. Some people may read it on a daily basis calling this their daily devotion and sometimes they will have a devotional book to go along with the Bible reading for that day but the problem that I see with this is that they will read the devotional before they will read the Scriptures. Listen my friends if you really want to study the Word of God you have to read it I encourage everyone to read through the Scriptures once a year. I believe it is important to be able to read the Scriptures and to study the Scriptures and to meditate upon those Scriptures so that we can know what the will of God is for our lives. No matter how interesting our daily devotional guides are, there is no substitute for the Scriptures.

Secondly - can you say commitment? Another condition for an in depth Bible study is commitment. Listen, we can commit to anything and everything that we so desire to do, but usually Bible study is not one of them.

Several years ago while attending liberty Bible Institute I had to take a required course called hermeneutics, which is a five-dollar word, and basically means how to interpret the Bible. Hermeneutics lays the groundwork for interpreting Scripture. There are some basic tools that I use even today in studying passages of Scripture. In sermon preparation there are certain things that I need to know, such as when was this written, to whom was it written what are the circumstances preceding this passage, what is this passage saying to me? With all this in mind let me try and show you a practical way of studying the Scriptures.

Hermeneutics simply means the application of reason in *how* to interpret the actual, intended meaning of a passage. Then, the principles of exegesis are put into practice, using the science and art of understanding to interpret the Bible for Christ's glory and not ours. In this way, we gain not just what it said then, but what the passage means for us today. So then we can come to His word, seek what it actually means, and then transcribe His timeless principles for today. I like to use the inductive method for studying the Bible.

Inductive Bible Study is a method for learning how to exegete (explain or interpret) the Bible for all its worth by our best efforts. We do this through learning the text and using the tools and skills that we have to help us rightfully divide the text, get in and dig out the meaning, and then of course apply it to our lives. There are several essential questions that we must ask ourselves when using the inductive method of interpretation. These questions are as follows.

The Essential Inductive Questions

1. What does this passage say?
2. What does this passage mean?
3. What is God telling me?
    4. How am I encouraged and strengthened by this passage?
    5. Is their any unconfessed sin in my life for which confession and repentance is needed?
    6. How will this passage change me, so I can learn and grow?
    7. What is in the way of these precepts affecting me? What is in the way of my listening to God?
    8. How does this apply to me? What am I going to do about it?
    9. What can I model in this text and how can I teach it?
    10. What does God want me to share with someone?

Combining the Inductive and Exegetical is simply using the best of both approaches to enhance our ability to study, know, and practice His Word. The idea of exegetical analysis is addition and complementing, to add what is missing from most Inductive approaches so to enhance our leaning and teaching.

Along with interpreting Scripture there are some tools that you need to help along in your study.

1. A good translation of the Bible
   2. A good Bible dictionary
   3. A good Bible concordance such as (Strong's concordance)
   4. A good commentary on the subject. Also make sure that the author of your commentary is someone that is credible and knows the Scriptures.

These are just some of the basic tools that will help you get started interpreting the Scriptures for your own spiritual gain.

There are other methods as well, but this is the one that I generally use. There are several books that have been written on the subject of Bible study, or studying the Bible for your self.

R.A. Torrey has written a book on the method of Bible study, Tim LaHaye has written a book How to study the Bible for yourself, and Kay Arthur has written a book How to study the Bible using the inductive method. I have looked at each of these writings and I must say Kay Arthur has done an outstanding job putting the framework together for studying the Bible. Hopefully if you are serious about studying the Bible and in gaining knowledge for yourself these books and methods will be a tremendous help.

In our quest to understand the doctrine of eternal security we must also look at some other crucial doctrines of the Bible. It is inevitable that all Christians whether of Baptist denomination, charismatic or any other denomination must understand and adhere to these doctrines, therefore we shall start with the doctrine of salvation. Let us begin by trying to get a clear understanding of salvation and the need to be saved.

Chapter 2

The Doctrine of Salvation

When I look around this old crazy world in which we live I have to wonder how people could and do get along in this world without Jesus. I wonder how could we? We live our lives as though there is no tomorrow we live for the here and now and are not worried about the consequences of our sins. The Bible is very clear when it states that all have sinned and come short of the glory of God.

When Adam fell in the garden he became a sinner and all those who are descendents after Adam are sinners. That puts you and me in that category, it is our nature to sin. We are not sinners because we sin, we sin because we are sinners I hope that, that statement makes sense to you, we are sinners because that is our nature that we have inherited it as a result of Adam's falling into sin in the Garden of Eden, and if we continue living our lives that way we will be doomed to a devil's hell.

I think we must get an unparalleled biblical understanding of what it meant and still means that Jesus left his riches in glory and humbled himself and became a servant and was willing to die upon the cross for you as He did for me. I believe that Paul answers these and other pertinent questions associated with the incarnation of Jesus Christ. The Bible declares that He came to seek and to save that which is lost (Luke 19:10).

Jesus was more than just a teacher He was the Prince of glory He came into the world to save sinners.

We have all sinned before a Holy and just God. We are sinful by nature the Bible tells us that there is none that seeketh after God. Those that do not have a personal relationship with Jesus Christ do not know Him and therefore cannot experience all the provisions that were accomplished upon the cross of Calvary. Without the provisions of the cross the sinner is helpless, hopeless and doomed. Jesus paid the sin debt with his own precious blood. The Bible says "There is no other name under heaven given among men whereby we must be saved" (Acts 4:12). Life really is doom and gloom without Christ. There is no future if salvation is neglected or rejected there can be no escape from the righteous judgment of God. God doesn't hide anything about sin, His righteousness or His judgment. Everything we need to know about salvation is found in the Bible.We need to take this subject very seriously, God has laid the ground rules for getting into heaven and it is only by blood of Jesus.

Therefore to answer the question "who needs salvation?" The answer should be very obvious. Each and every person that has ever lived, is living, or will live has a need to be saved simply because we are all sinners. We stand guilty before a holy and just God. So if we just keep on doing what we're doing now Hebrews chapter 2: 3 become a reality in our life.

In Hebrews chapter 2:3 it says [3] How shall we escape, if we neglect so great salvation; which at the first began to be spoken by the Lord, and was confirmed unto us by them that heard him;

The writer of Hebrews warns us about neglecting the salvation which is related to sin. Salvation through Jesus Christ is perhaps one of the greatest manifestations of God's power. We are made righteous we are justified in the eyes of God. God's power has set us free from Satanic bondage, the bondage of sin which is made possible only through the death and resurrection of Jesus Christ. Salvation is not just a new phase of Christianity or religion but it is dateless in the mind of God. Even before the foundations of the world were put into motion God, his Son Jesus and the Holy Spirit conceived in their minds the eternal purpose of salvation. (Eph. 3:11 "According to the eternal purpose which He purposed in Christ Jesus our Lord:"

(Titus 1:2 In hope of eternal life, which God, that cannot lie, promised before the world began).

It all began with God's foreknowledge that He foresaw the need for salvation even before the world was spinning on its axis. Even before the creation of man God looked into the heart of man and saw a sinful depraved heart. Look at what the scriptures declare about salvation.

Romans 5:8 - But God commendeth his love toward us, in that, while we were yet sinners, Christ died for us.

Eph. 1:4 - According as he hath chosen us in him before the foundation of the world, that we should be holy and without blame before him in love:

Sometimes we forget that salvation is not in something, but Someone.

Isa. 12:2

Behold, God is my salvation; I will trust, and not be afraid: for the LORD JEHOVAH is my strength and my song; he also is become my salvation.

Ps. 12:1

The LORD is my light and my salvation; whom shall I fear? the LORD is the strength of my life; of whom shall I be afraid?

If we think of salvation as something tangible, something that we must struggle with from day to day or moment to moment to try and keep, then I believe that we would be in constant fear of losing our salvation, remember our salvation is not in something tangible but it is in Christ and Christ alone. The Bible say's that it is ridiculous to try and keep our salvation when we did absolutely nothing to get it or earn it, it's a free gift of God, and He is the savior and the keeper (Eph. 2:8-9).

The subject of salvation is one of those that we need to look at from a logical standpoint. I realize that there is nothing logical about salvation and we don't really understand how it works but we do know that God so loved us that He allowed His only begotten Son to die upon the cross so that you and I could be saved. One of the greatest fears is that not all Christians understand or comprehend the fullness of salvation. Perhaps in some people's minds salvation is limited to what takes place when we accept Christ or invite Him to be our savior. There are a lot of Christians who at the point of salvation are thankful that they are saved and that their sins are forgiven, but once again that may be as far they take it.

What the New Testament Teaches about Salvation

But the New Testament actually teaches "I have been saved, I am being saved, I have yet to be saved". It is important for us to recognize these three aspects of salvation. Before we get into these three all-important aspects of salvation I would like for us to go back to our life before we were saved. Even before the foundations of the world God, sitting upon His throne with His Beloved Son sitting next to Him, conceived in their minds that there was going to be a need for salvation. Before we get too far ahead of ourselves, lets look and get the definition of what "salvation" means.

Vines Expository Dictionary

sal•va•tion \sal-□vā-shən\ noun
1   **a** : deliverance from the power and effects of sin
       b : the agent or means that effects salvation

    c : Christian Science **:** the realization of the supremacy of
       infinite Mind over all bringing with it the destruction of
       the illusion of sin, sickness, and death
2   **:** liberation from ignorance or illusion
3   **a :** preservation from destruction or failure
    b : deliverance from danger or difficulty

(Vines Bible dic.)

    In God's foreknowledge he saw the wickedness of a
depraved heart and the sinfulness of man. Some people believe
that divine salvation is from God and God only, and there
are others who believe it is by God plus something else. That
something else can be baptism, church membership, being
a tither, or even knocking on doors, most people just cannot
grasp the concept that salvation is as simple as believing
God. God's perfect salvation dealt with our past, includes our
present, as well as our future. Take these next three versus for
example they do not speak of three different types of salvation
but simply three different aspects of one salvation.

(Philippians 2:12) [12] Wherefore, my beloved, as ye have
always obeyed, not as in my presence only, but now much
more in my absence, <u>work out your own salvation with fear
and trembling.</u>

(Romans 13: 11) And that, knowing the time, that now it is
high time to awake out of sleep: <u>for now is our salvation nearer
than when we believed</u>

(II Timothy 1:9) <u>Who hath saved us, and called us with an
holy calling</u>, not according to our works, but according to his
own purpose and grace, which was given us in Christ Jesus
before the world began

    It is important that we learned to be able to discern the
difference. Maybe you never thought of it in this fashion, but
we know that salvation is an accomplished fact from eternity
past and that the Holy Spirit which lives within us is saving us
even now and He is keeping us saved for the future. In order

to get a clear understanding of the concept we must learn that salvation is an accomplished fact, it already happened. The moment we accept Christ as Lord and Savior we are saved, but we must take it two steps further. We are being saved even now by the power of the Holy Ghost it is a here and now process and if we take it to the next phase we are being saved for the future, in other words for eternity. Let us look back to the past to see what took place as far as our salvation is concerned.

Salvation Past

Salvation is a gift from God that we receive the moment we accept God's Son Jesus Christ as our Lord and Savior. (Rom. 1:16) For I am not ashamed of the gospel of Christ: <u>for it is the power of God unto salvation to every one that believeth;</u> to the Jew first, and also to the Greek . As I said earlier a lot of people have a hard time understanding or believing that one can be saved just by believing God. That is exactly what the bible teaches, salvation is unto all or everyone that believes. No matter how sinful we were in our past the blood of Jesus clearly wiped those sins away. (Isaiah 1:18) Come now, and let us reason together, saith the LORD: though your sins be as scarlet, they shall be as white as snow; though they be red like crimson, they shall be as wool. Adrian Rogers once said and I quote "there is no one so bad he can not be saved and no one so good he need not be saved."

The reason we need salvation to start with is because sin had entered into the world, if it were not for sin then we would not need a Savior. Because Adam fell in the garden we too have come under the curse and condemnation of God's judgment. (I Cor. 15:22) For as in Adam all die, even so in Christ shall all be made alive.

(Rom. 5:18) Therefore as by the offence of one judgment came upon all men to condemnation; even so by the righteousness of one the free gift came upon all men unto justification of life.

Most people think that they are able to stand in front of God unashamed but the Bible clearly tells us that without Christ we are alienated against God because of our sin. In all actuality we are the enemies of God without Christ.

(Rom. 5:1) ¹ Therefore being justified by faith, we have peace with God through our Lord Jesus Christ.

When we come to Christ and accept Him as Lord and Savior then we have made peace with God. Salvation is an accomplished fact. Look at these passages of Scripture's that go along with this theology.

(Luke 7:50) Thy faith hath saved thee; go in peace

(Ephesians 2: 8) For by grace are ye saved through faith; and that not of yourselves: it is the gift of God:

(Titus 3:5) Not by works of righteousness which we have done, but according to his mercy he saved us, by the washing of regeneration, and renewing of the Holy Ghost;

Salvation Present

Now let's look at the second aspect of salvation what I like to call the present process. The Holy Spirit at work in our lives. Because it is a personal salvation it becomes effective as we recognize it as a present salvation. (II Corinthians 6: 2) (For he saith, I have heard thee in a time accepted, and in the day of salvation have I succoured thee: behold, now is the accepted time; behold, now is the day of salvation.)

(Luke 19:9) And Jesus said unto him, This day is salvation come to this house, forsomuch as he also is a son of Abraham.

When God says, "Now" he means "Now" or this very moment. It is a very foolish thing to look at salvation as something that we must work for or earn it in some way or another. When we have to labor for our salvation then it becomes a chore but not only is it a chore we come away with a vague hope that we will be saved. If you are a child of God you are being saved even right now. Look at the Scripture references.

(I Corinthians 1:18) For the preaching of the cross is to them that perish foolishness; but unto <u>us which are saved</u> it is the power of God

(Hebrews 10:39) But we are not of them who draw back unto perdition; but of them that <u>believe to the saving of the soul.</u>

You ask a person if they are saved and most of the time you'll get a response such as "Oh yes I was saved and baptized on such and such day". Most of the time people can give you time and place where their salvation became a reality but once again that's as far as they take it. I believe that it is a wonderful thing to know when we were saved, but if we look at it from a biblical standpoint and our theology is correct then we must also incorporate I am being saved even as we speak.

Eternity Future

(Hebrews 1: 14) Are they not all ministering spirits, sent forth to minister for them who shall be heirs of salvation.

(James 1: 21) Wherefore lay apart all filthiness and superfluity of naughtiness, and receive with meekness the engrafted word, <u>which is able to save your souls.</u>

(I Peter 1:5) Who are kept by the power of God through <u>faith unto salvation</u> ready to be revealed in the last time.

The apostle Paul must have had the future in mind when he gave us this third aspect of salvation.

(Romans 13:11) And that, knowing the time, that now it is high time to awake out of sleep: <u>for now is our salvation nearer than when we believed.</u>

Peter speaks of this aspect of salvation also as being "ready to be revealed in the last Time" (I Peter 1:5). What does this verse mean that our salvation is nearer than when we first believed? That is an interesting statement is it not? Did we not receive salvation the moment we believed? Of course we did and we continue to receive salvation as we believe. Then if we receive salvation at the moment we believed what is Paul talking about when he says it is nearer than we believed? I believe what Paul is talking about is this it is salvation from the presence of sin, just as salvation in past delivered us from the penalty of sin, a present salvation delivers us from the power of sin. In essence what Paul is saying here is that Christ is our salvation and the return of Christ is closer now than when we first believed.

I hope that I have cleared up this all important subject of salvation, and why we all need to be saved. Remember eternity is just a heartbeat away. If you have never asked Christ to forgive you of your sins and to cleanse you from all unrighteousness now would be an appropriate time to do that.

Chapter 3

What about Grace?

GRACE, Undeserved acceptance and love received from another, especially the characteristic attitude of God in providing salvation for sinners. For Christians, the word "grace" is virtually synonymous with the gospel of God's gift of unmerited salvation in Jesus Christ. To express this, the New Testament writers used the Greek word charis, which had a long previous history in secular Greek. Related to the word for joy or pleasure, charis originally referred to something delightful or attractive in a person, something which brought pleasure to others. From this it came to have the idea of a favor or kindness done to another or of a gift which brought pleasure to another. Viewed from the standpoint of the recipient, it was used to refer to the thankfulness felt for a gift or favor. These meanings also appear in the biblical use of charis, but only in the New Testament does it come to have the familiar sense which "grace" bears for Christians.
(Holman Bible dictionary)

I believe that the Scriptures are very clear. We are saved by God's grace and not of our selves. We could never save ourselves no matter what the circumstances were. Salvation is a free gift from God. We haven't earned a gift nor do we deserve a gift.

God's gifts should prompt the proper response from the recipients. This response includes not boasting (1 Cor. 4:7; Eph. 2:8); amazement at God's inexpressible goodness (2 Cor. 9:15); the using of gifts for the furtherance of Christ's kingdom (1 Tim. 4:14; 2 Tim. 1:6-11); and a life of good works (Eph. 2:10).

Holman Bible Dictionary

Grace has been described as "God's riches at Christ's expense". Grace is unmerited and undeserved favor. The word grace and its cognates, "gracious" and "graciously" occur in the Scriptures almost 200 times. In order to get the right concept of eternal security we must have a clear understanding of what grace really is. If we do not understand this fundamental truth of grace then of course the other doctrines of the Bible including eternal security will not be understood either. Salvation, sanctification, justification are all associated with God's grace. I love this acronym of grace.

G = God's
R = riches
A = at
C = Christ's
E = expense

I can remember the first time that I saw this acronym, since then I have never looked at or even thought of grace in the same manner. Grace really cost God everything. Not only did Grace cost God His Son's life, but grace is also the result of the resurrection of Jesus. Not only was it by God's grace that Jesus resurrected from the dead but it was, and still is, grace that put Jesus back upon the throne sitting at the right hand of our Heavenly Father, and what is He doing, but making intercession for the Saints.

We cannot work our way into heaven, buy our way into heaven or be good enough to get into heaven. We certainly can't boast our way into heaven. I remember several years ago there was a song out by Elvis Presley "I did it my way". If we do it our way we will surely end up in the pits of hell. There is only one way and that is God's way. The conclusion is this- we cannot earn eternal life. Is eternal security biblical? You be the judge or should I say let the bible be the judge. I believe that one can fall from grace, but if one is a genuine Christian he can never fall out of grace. In other words what I am saying is that he can never lose his salvation! Christ makes the promise to us in John chapter 10:28-29 that we are eternally secure in him.

²⁸ And I give unto them eternal life; and they shall never perish, neither shall any man pluck them out of my hand. ²⁹ My Father, which gave them me, is greater than all; and no man is able to pluck them out of my Father's hand.

It has been well said, that grace is unmerited and undeserved favor, grace is the unlimited favor to the undeserving. You and I have far removed ourselves from the divine favor of God because we have transgressed against a holy God. Therefore grace truly is undeserved unmerited favor. Perhaps one of the greatest things about grace is that it is absolutely free. It is free to the transgressors, but it cost God everything. God in his foreknowledge knew that we were going to have to experience grace so that we might inherit the kingdom of God. Jesus then left Heaven's glory and all the riches there to humble himself and to become a man, but much more than just a man He was the God man. Jesus was 100% God, yet He was 100% man. He experienced all the temptations that you and I experience every day yet he was sinless.

Phil. 2:5-8

Let this mind be in you, which was also in Christ Jesus: ⁶ Who, being in the form of God, thought it not robbery to be equal with God: ⁷ But made himself of no reputation, and took upon him the form of a servant, and was made in the likeness of men: [8] And being found in fashion as a man, he humbled himself, and became obedient unto death, even the death of the cross.

Since we are on the subject of grace I think many people get the wrong idea of what grace really is. Grace comes to us through Christ (John 1:17; 1: 14). Here the apostle makes it very clear that grace would be personified in Christ. Once again, if we do not understand the concept of grace and it's clear meaning well, then the other fundamentals of the Scripture cannot be understood either.

Was Abraham justified by works?

Romans 4:1-2

[1] What shall we say then that Abraham our father, as pertaining to the flesh, hath found?

[2] For if Abraham were justified by works, he hath whereof to glory; but not before God.

Paul begins by asking, what then shall we say that Abraham, our forefather according to the flesh, has found? He was asking the question because the Jews questioned the idea about Abraham's righteousness. Much like today we have the same problem, people want to be justified by their works and not by the faith that they place in the Lord Jesus Christ. Abraham's righteousness was not imputed to him by his works but his faith in the true and living God. Like Paul, Abraham was sovereignly and directly chosen by God. Neither Abraham nor Paul were searching for God when they were divinely called and commissioned. Abraham may have never heard of the true God. Living in the land of Ur, Abraham grew up worshiping idols and practicing paganism. Paul on the other hand was enjoying persecuting Christians thinking that he was pleasing God with his life. But I think as it always is the case with true belief, when the Holy Spirit convicts you, He also as He did with Abraham's mind and heart enlightens us to recognize the one true and only God.

The Bible says that if Abraham was justified by works then of course he would have something to boast about. But not before God. The only thing that Abraham did to find favor with God was to obey in faith to God.

I could probably devote a whole chapter on Abraham's faith, but I won't. There is however one thing that I would like for us to see before we move on. In Romans chapter 4 and verse number three the bible says.

"For what saith the scripture? Abraham believed God, and it was reckoned unto him for righteousness".

I would like for us to look at this word **reckoned** the Greek word is from logizomai which carries the economic and legal meaning of crediting something to another's account. The only thing God received from Abraham was his imperfect faith, but by His divine grace and mercy, He reckoned it to Abraham's spiritual account as righteousness.

The Bible says by faith Abraham believed God and it was credited to his spiritual account as righteousness. You and I must come to God in the same way by faith and it is by this faith that we are saved and sealed until the day of redemption. Are we going to allow our weak theology and shallow thinking to place a limit on God? That would be a vital mistake on our part. The doctrine of grace is important to understand. As we consider that it is only by God's grace that we can be saved. In order to do justice to the doctrine of grace.

Chapter 4

Adoption

One difficulty that we have today is that we have a hard time understanding the doctrine of adoption. Most people would say that you cannot be born and adopted into the same family. That is our modern concept of course in speaking on a physical realm. Let's look on the biblical realm of adoption. Lets go beyond our human conception of adoption. Our human ideology does not allow us to get past this human philosophy.

A preacher friend of mine who was allowed to preach in my church one time when I was gone preached against the subject of adoption. Needless to say that was the last time that he preached in my church. The Bible teaches that we are both born into the family of God and we are also adopted into the family of God. This is the way it works God adopts those into his family who have been born again. Let's start by looking at this Greek word for adoption huiothesia—Strong's a compound of words "son" and "a placing," meaning not the putting into a place of a child, but the putting into place of a son. If we look at it in a biblical sense the word of adoption implies change of nature change of relationship. Sonship always precedes adoption. What I mean by that is this you have to be born again to know Jesus Christ as Lord and Savior before you can be adopted into God's family.

In order to get a clearer meaning of adoption we must take the approach from the Roman law. I am by no means an authority on Roman law but this is my understanding of it. A Roman family from a legal standpoint consisted of a head or a ruler, of the persons subject to his absolute power. The lawful children of the head of the family were in his power, as also were persons unconnected with him by blood if they had been brought into his power by the artificial tie of adoption. Sometimes marriages do not produce children and sometimes the sons went to the grave before the father and if that was the case then there would be no heir to the estate. In order to keep the family from being extinct the head of the family would either have to adopt himself to another family or else he would have to adopt a son who would perpetuate his own family. 'Adoption is an act of God's free grace, whereby we are received into the number, and have a right to all the privileges of the sons of God' (Shorter Catechism, Question 34).

Chapter 5

The Doctrine of Predestination

All students of the Bible from time to time come up against apparent problems in their quest for knowledge of the Word of God. This doctrine of predestination could perhaps be one of those problems. Most of the time we can take the word of God, read it, and study and meditate upon it and its simplicity. Sometimes as we study the Word of God it should be studied carefully with much prayer and meditation upon the passage in which we study. This doctrine of predestination seems to be one of those problematic truths. This is one of those doctrines that many books have been written about, it is also a doctrine that separates many of God's people. One of the reasons why this doctrine separates many of God's children is the simple fact that we are not secure in our faith.

Perhaps another reason we don't understand the doctrine of predestination is the fact that we don't understand the sovereignty of God. There appears to be a whole host of words that are closely associated with the sovereignty of God, three of those words that we are going to look at in this chapter are the words foreknowledge, election, and predestination. Because of who and what God is He is able to do as He wills, God being omniscient knows everything, but not only does He know everything about eternity past He also knows everything about eternity future and God has devised a divine plan. His providences are ordered and ordained into every facet of life. Predestination is the result of God's will, predestination is a result of God's grace and His love. God can never be guilty of anything capricious for He is sovereign and Holy and He ordained it before the foundations of the world. Dr. C.I. Schofield puts it this way.

"The divine order is foreknowledge, election, predestination. That foreknowledge determines the election or choice is clear, I Peter 1:2, Elect according to the foreknowledge of God the Father, through sanctification of the Spirit, unto obedience and sprinkling of the blood of Jesus Christ: Grace unto you, and peace, be multiplied. and predestination is the bringing to pass of the election. Election looks back to foreknowledge: predestination forward to the destiny. But Scripture nowhere declares that it is in the divine foreknowledge which determines the divine election and predestination. The foreknown are elected, and the elected are predestined, and this election is certain to every believer by the mere fact that he believes." (I Thessalonians 1: 4, 5) Knowing, brethren beloved, your election of God. ⁵ For our gospel came not unto you in word only, but also in power, and in the Holy Ghost, and in much assurance; as ye know what manner of men we were among you for your sake.

One very important fact that I must bring to mind is the fact that predestination is not God's pre-determining from eternity past who should and who should not be saved. The Scriptures do not teach this view. But what in fact it does teach is that this doctrine of predestination has everything to do with eternity future of all believers.

The Foreknowledge of God

What an awesome word "fore" or "before" it simply means that God knows beforehand what the future holds. How awesome is that when you think about the omniscience of God, He knows the beginning from the end and the end from the beginning. Nothing is hidden from God. The Bible says that God knows what we have need of even before we ask Him. God in His foreknowledge set our salvation in motion even before the foundations of the world were laid.

The Greek word for foreknowledge is proginosko. The medical word prognosis is connected to this word. Prognosis is a prediction concerning the future course of disease, based on diagnosis. This word does not appear in the Old Testament but appears seven times in the New Testament, and it relates to God's foreknowledge. The word foreknowledge does not appear in the Old Testament, but when the word, "know" is used in connection with God, it means to "choose" or "set favor upon" or "acknowledge." It is those whom he chose or set his favor upon. Here are some texts to show this meaning of "knowing."

"I know you by name" (Exodus 33:17) "Before I formed you in the womb, I knew you." (Jeremiah 1:5) "You have been rebellious against the Lord from the day I knew you." (Deut. 9:24) Romans 11: 2, Gen.18:17-19, Hosea 13:4-5, 1 Cor. 8:3, 2 Tim. 2:16-19

Whom he fore knew he also predestined," means that God appointed the destiny of his people, based on his prior election, and this election is not based on any foreseen faith that we could produce.

Romans 8:28-30

And we know that God causes all things to work together for good to those who love God, to those who are called according to His purpose. 29) For whom He fore knew, He also predestined to become conformed to the image of His Son, that He might be the first-born among many brethren; 30) and whom He predestined, these He also called; and whom He called, these He also justified; and whom He justified, these He also glorified.

'For' indicates that verses 29-30 are the foundation for verse 28. They give reasons why we can <u>KNOW</u> all things will work together for good to those who are called according to God's purpose. In these few verses, we see the great doctrines of election and predestination and effectual calling and justification and glorification.

Chapter 6

Election

What another great doctrine! This doctrine teaches that all those who are divinely chosen cannot and will not ever perish. For they were chosen in Christ Jesus before the foundations of the world before sin entered the world. Therefore those that have come to know Jesus Christ as Lord and Savior will never perish just as the Bible says. God's elected can do nothing to destroy God's eternal purpose. All who are saved are the vessels of God's mercy. Rom. 9:23: And that he might make known the riches of his glory on the vessels of mercy, which he had afore prepared unto glory,

Ephesians 1: 3-11 Blessed be the God and Father of our Lord Jesus Christ, who hath blessed us with all spiritual blessings in heavenly places in Christ: [4] According as he hath chosen us in him before the foundation of the world, that we should be holy and without blame before him in love: [5] Having predestinated us unto the adoption of children by Jesus Christ to himself, according to the good pleasure of his will, [6] To the praise of the glory of his grace, wherein he hath made us accepted in the beloved. [7] In whom we have redemption through his blood, the forgiveness of sins, according to the riches of his grace; [8] Wherein he hath abounded toward us in all wisdom and prudence; [9] Having made known unto us the mystery of his will, according to his good pleasure which he hath purposed in himself: [10] That in the dispensation of the fulness of times he might gather together in one all things in Christ, both which are in heaven, and which are on earth; even in him: [11] In whom also we have obtained an inheritance, being predestinated according to the purpose of him who worketh all things after the counsel of his own will:

What a glorious truth we are about to expound on. In verse three of this passage Paul says blessed be the God and Father of our Lord Jesus Christ who hath blessed us with all spiritual blessings in heavenly places in Christ. Now look at the phrase "According as" in verse number four. This is as real as it gets as far as pertaining to predestination, election and the adoption of sons. Stay with me for a minute as we look into this passage. "According as" is a connective which modifies the preceding statement in verse three. The spiritual blessings that you and I receive come from the divine will of God and it is all done for God's purpose to please Him to bring glory and honor to Him. The Bible says that we should bless God (that is to eulogize God) because He has blessed us with all spiritual blessings in heavenly places in Christ. There should be three ins in verse three. It should be that we are blessed in all spiritual blessings in heavenly places in Christ. The thought is this that we should open our eyes and see what God has done for us. All of this was done because God had a plan the Word says He chose us in Him before the foundation of the world. God chose us before the foundations of the world He had a plan and a purpose for each and everyone of us.

Therefore, if God had chosen us to be saved why would He then un-choose us to be saved? Why would He allow us to give back such a precious gift if He had chosen us before the foundations of the world. He chose us so that we should be holy and without blame before Him in love. It was His love for us that caused God to predestinate us. The apostle Paul goes on and says having predestinated us unto the adoption of children by Jesus Christ to Himself according to the good pleasure of His will. What does this verse mean?

John 1:12 But as many as received him, to them gave he power to become the sons of God, even to them that believe on his name:

This verse says when we receive Christ as Lord and Savior "as many as received Him" He gave us power to become sons of God. That is to say that we have been adopted as sons and daughters into the family of God by what Jesus Christ did on the cross. If we have been adopted by God according to God's perfect will and we are heirs to the throne of God. We are in God's family part of a family and I just don't see any reason why God would go through all that trouble of electing us and then predestinated us to be saved for nothing. Essentially that's what it would be if we could throw our salvation away. It would be good for nothing. Most people believe that we have a free will to choose whether or not we will be saved.

Chapter 7

Eternal security: Is it biblical?

The question has been around since the inception of grace. That age-old question, can one truly lose one's salvation? I hope to answer that question in this section. When I was doing research for this project, I couldn't find much information out there as a way of defending the doctrine of eternal security or preservation of the saints which ever you want to call it. The Southern Baptist Convention Baptist Faith and Message calls it election under article V **God's purpose of grace** and says that all true believers will persevere to the end.

I am inclined to agree with that statement. However, when contacting our seminaries and not getting any phone calls back, I have to wonder what is being taught to our young preachers. I called Covington Theological Seminary of which may I say that I am a proud graduate and glad to be associated with such a fine seminary. I talked to Dr. Hutchings and ask his view on eternal security he told me that they were aligned with the Southern Baptist Faith and Message,and they are indeed affiliated with the Southern Baptist Convention although I don't think that the Southern Baptist acknowledge them as such. I was so pleased to hear that the school that I had attended for so many years still holds a doctrinal truth God's Word firm in their hands and hearts. I found when contacting other seminaries and the Bible colleges many of which are afraid to take a stand because they might offend some. I have to conclude that perhaps bible training in some seminaries is all about money and not about teaching God's Word. There are many schools who claim to be nondenominational therefore they cannot take a stand one way or the other. However that is taking the easy way out. We have grown accustomed in this country to try to please everybody we do not want to offend anyone. God's Word is offensive and if we take Him at His word it will offend those who are not in agreement with God's Word.

I am a graduate of Masters Graduate School of Divinity where I earned my Doctor of Divinity degree, I talked with Dr. Fry on the phone who is the president of Masters, on this all important subject. I am in agreement with him when he says that when a person is genuinely saved he cannot lose his salvation. Of course we don't know when salvation becomes a reality in their life. That is a matter between that person and God. We can't really say for sure if a person is saved, but there sure needs to be evidence of a changed live. We may not be their judge but we certainly are to be fruit inspectors.

I do not believe in a gospel that can be built to suit all our needs.I think that we as Christians either have to stand for something or else we will fall for anything.I think that God makes it very clear in the Scriptures that we are secure with our salvation in Christ Jesus.

I know that a lot of our young men coming out of seminary have not been taught this vital doctrine of truth. Southern Baptist pastors do not proclaim it from our pulpits. It is like a lost doctrine of the Bible. What do I mean that it is a lost doctrine? What I truly mean, is that it has been lost between the pages of the Bible.I think that's why sometimes preachers do not take a stand one way or the other on eternal security they skim the pages of the Bible and when they come across hard teachings they bypass them not knowing where they stand one way or the other. It seems to me that we have a lack of commitment from those who are teaching the Word of God to say "thus saith the Lord". If the Lord says that he has sealed us until the day of redemption, don't you think that we should proclaim that from our pulpits?

To some it is a most discouraging doctrine. The reason I say that it is most discouraging to some is for the simple fact that we want to add works to salvation. Most people want to take this doctrine lightly because they want to add to salvation. People think that they have to help God keep us saved. When God was designing the universe and man I don't believe that he ask any of us about salvation and what we needed to do in order to be saved or to stay saved. My intention and purpose for writing this book is to give a simple but biblical explanation on eternal security.

When people come to know Jesus Christ as Lord and Savior, they are brought into a relationship that guarantees their eternal security. In the Bible the book of Jude declares, "<u>Now unto him that is able to keep you from falling, and to present you faultless before the presence of his glory with exceeding joy,</u>" God's power is able to keep the believer from falling. It is up to God and not us, to present us before His glorious presence. Our eternal security is the result of God keeping us, and not us trying to do whatever we can to maintain our own salvation.

The Lord Jesus Christ proclaimed, "I give unto them eternal life, and they shall never perish; no one can snatch them out of my hand. My Father who has given them to me, is greater than all, and no one can snatch them out of my Father's hand" (John 10:28-29). The Lord Jesus Christ and God the Father have us tightly gripped in their hands so no one including ourselves is able to separate us from the love of God.

As a pastor in rural Missouri. The question has come up within my own congregation as well. I have addressed this question several times. I have had people in my own congregation, come and tell me that they did not trust the doctrine of eternal security. Most of the time people that question the idea of eternal security are perhaps the same people that do not have the assurance of salvation. This is a topic that we shall talk about in more depth later on. Most people believe that this doctrine gives people a license to sin this of course is another topic that we will address later on down the road as well. My congregation is not very big and knowing if it comes up in our small congregations and if I don't deal with the question from a biblical perspective, then I have failed as a pastor. One thing that I want to make very clear is that I can never persuade anyone to change their viewpoint on any doctrine or any- thing pertaining to Scripture unless the Holy Spirit intercedes. One thing that I know for sure is that people have their own opinion whether it be right or wrong, biblical or not biblical. Most of the time when you present them with a scriptural viewpoint of doctrinal truth, most will continue to be believe what he or she already believes. The truth of the matter is our congregations are full of carnal people that do not or will not adhere to what the Word of God has to say. What about pastors of bigger or mega churches that don't have any idea of what is being taught in there Sunday school classes? I know for a fact there are Southern Baptist churches in my area that Sunday school teachers and perhaps even pastors do not believe or teach eternal security. You probably have gotten the idea by now that I am a Southern Baptist pastor and you are right in your assumption. This book however is not intended for Southern Baptist entirely. I would like to plead my case to those who are not sure what they believe about eternal security.

How many sins must I sin before I lose my salvation?

I had to ask myself the question, if I could lose my salvation by sinning I wonder which sin will send me to hell?

Would it be a so-called big sin, or would it be some little sin that I just forgot to confess. Would it be a sin of omission or a sin of co-mission. I wonder if at the moment I got saved and had a filthy thought or a greedy thought or anything of that nature would I go to hell? When Jesus died on the cross which sins did he forgive me of? Those are some good questions I hope that I have the answers to those questions. When you ask someone these questions, especially those who do not believe the doctrine of eternal security, which sin would it be that sends them to hell, you get a variety of answers. In my humble opinion I think that they are theologically off-base. I asked someone the question, "if by chance you were able to lose your salvation which sin would send you to hell?" The reply was this, "it depends on how major the sin was." That is the problem because we try to put sins in categories. Major sins and not so major sins, come on let's get real. Sin is sin and sin is sin no matter how we look at it. Another person says that it will be the last sin that you commit that will send you to hell. I am not very comfortable with that statement the because we sin multiple times every day. What if I die before I have a chance to confess my last sin. Then I must drift away into a devil's hell?

Let's look at that first question. If I could lose my salvation by sinning which sin would send me to hell? It would have to be the first sin I commit after salvation that would send me to hell. If that's the case. Sin is sin in the eyes of God, it doesn't matter what we consider big or small, o-mission or co-mission. We have a tendency of putting sin in categories I think you know what I mean. We might say something like,"he told a little white lie," or "that is a gray area between right and wrong" and we don't really come out and say it is sin. If God was going to send you to hell anyway, why would he allow his only begotten Son to die on a cruel cross to begin with? I think in speaking from a theological viewpoint that there is only one sin that will send a person to hell. That is the rejection of Jesus

Christ the Son of God as your Lord and Savior. Either Jesus could forgive all sins past, present, and future or he could not forgive any. There are some that will argue this point saying that there are eternal sins and if you commit the sins after you have gotten saved you certainly die and go to a devil's hell. One of the scripture reference that they use is found in I Cor. 6:9-11

[9] Know ye not that the unrighteous shall not inherit the kingdom of God? Be not deceived: neither fornicators, nor idolaters, nor adulterers, nor effeminate, nor abusers of themselves with mankind, [10] Nor thieves, nor covetous, nor drunkards, nor revilers, nor extortioners, shall inherit the kingdom of God. [11] And such were some of you: but ye are washed, but ye are sanctified, but ye are justified in the name of the Lord Jesus, and by the Spirit of our God.

In this passage Paul was talking to the church at Corinth because there was sin going on within the church. Christians were suing Christians and going before secular courts and not trying to work out their differences on their own or seeking spiritual guidance on such matters. So Paul was trying to correct the Corinthians in their spiritual weakness and reminds them that they too by the grace of God have come out of a lifestyle like Paul describes in the verses above. In verse 9 he says "Know ye not the unrighteous will not inherit the kingdom of God". The Kingdom is the spiritual sphere of salvation where God rules as king over all who belong to Him by faith. All believers are in this spiritual kingdom, yet are waiting to enter into the fulness of our inheritance in the age to come. People who are characterized by these indignations are not saved. It is important to understand that Christians can and do commit these sins. It just proves that we are living in a sinful world, and it proves that we are not in God's kingdom. I believe that when true believers commit these sins they must confess these sins before God and repent and receive victory over it. We cannot continue to live our lives in unconfessed sin, unconfessed sin breaks the fellowship that we have God.

What about the seal?

Every legal document in the world has some sort of a seal upon it. A birth certificates has a seal placed upon it signifying that you have been born into a family. Likewise our new birth in the spiritual realm has a seal placed upon it. Even the scroll that Jesus holds in his hand in the book of Revelation has been sealed.

Ephesians 4:30 tells us that believers are "sealed until the day of redemption." If believers do not have eternal life, then the sealing of the believer could not be until the day of redemption. The apostle must have mis- spoke, because if that is the case then the seal would be broken on the day we first sinned, or in the case of apostasy, or disbelief or whatever the nature would be that would cause us to fall out of grace. Jesus himself promised that whosoever believes in him would have everlasting life. If he can take it away from you or you can lose it yourself, or even give it back, then it's not eternal. Listen, if eternal security is not biblical and is not a true doctrine of the Bible then the Bible is wrong in offering eternal life. It would be wrong to get one's hope up, thinking they might have eternal life. Most of the time we want to put stipulations on eternal life, such as if I am good enough, if I do enough good works, if I am baptized, or if I speak in tounges the list could go on and on, or whatever stipulation you put on the work of God.

Perhaps one of the most convincing argument for eternal security is Romans 8:38-39 which simply says "For I am persuaded, that neither death, nor life, nor angels, nor principalities, nor powers, nor things present, nor things to come, [39] Nor height, nor depth, nor any other crea ture, shall be able to separate us from the love of God, which is in Christ Jesus our Lord".

Our eternal security is based on the love of God for those He has redeemed. Our eternal security was bought with the precious blood of Jesus Christ, promised by God the Father, and sealed by the Holy Spirit UNTIL THE DAY OF REDEMPTION! Man! it doesn't get any clearer than that.

I believe with all my heart that God has a plan and a purpose for each one of us. [28] And we know that all things work together for good to them that love God, to them who are the called according to his purpose. [29] For whom he did foreknow, he also did predestinate to be conformed to the image of his Son, that he might be the firstborn among many brethren. [30] Moreover whom he did predestinate, them he also called: and whom he called, them he also justified: and whom he justified, them he also glorified.
(Romans 8: 28 -30).

The work of the Father is to predestine all those He foreknew to be conformed to the image of His dear Son. Predestination means that, when God saves you, He is going to see you through. Whom He foreknew, He predestinated, and whom He predestinated, He called, and whom He called, He justified, and whom He justified, He glorified. What does this word predestination mean? The word means to determine before or ordain.

One of the most awesome truths in all the Bible is that of the foreknowledge of God. When I think about how God saw me and knew me before the foundation of the world. I have chills running up and down my spine. It is just an awesome thought that Jehovah God knew me before He created the universe. Think about it for a minute. If a God that awesome created the entire cosmos out of nothing, and wants to have a relationship with the ones that he created and wants us to know Him as well, then why do we want to put a limitation on his sovereignty and his omnipotent power?

We want to put God in a box, make Him a small god instead of making Him the God that He is. We always want to rationalize and look at God through man's eyes. The Bible says that God's ways and thoughts are much higher than ours. I guess I just don't understand why we would allow ourselves to make this doctrine much harder than it really is. In verse 24 of the book of Jude it say's "Now unto him that is able to keep you from falling, and to present you faultless before the presence of his glory with exceeding joy, [25] To the only wise God our Saviour, be glory and majesty, dominion and power, both now and forever. Amen."

This is the conclusion of Jude's short letter. Note that this is a benediction upon believers. It is perhaps one of the most well known benedictions by Christians all over the world. This great benediction tells us the source of the believer's security. What is the source of the believer's security? Who is it that keeps the believer secure while he walks upon the earth? It is God.

The Fear of Falling

There is a real fear that people are not going to live lives pleasing to God. If we have a shadow hanging over our heads all the time for the fear of failing to please God. If a person is scared to death about sinning and losing their salvation they cannot possibly be doing all that they can for the kingdom of God. Frankly I don't know how some people would be able to sleep at night not knowing if they committed some sin in their sleep that God would send them to hell.

My question is how is one to know what to say or how to defend your stance on such issues? I don't think that it is just this one issue of eternal security that people are confused about. Frankly I think our churches have failed when it comes to teaching strong biblical doctrines. Some of the doctrines that I feel that our churches have forgotten or have omitted to teach are those of Divine Inspiration that tells us that the Bible is the written or God breathed Word. How about the Trinity?

Some say that Jesus was just a man or a prophet. Some say He was a good man. Let me put it to you this way, if Jesus was not who He said He is, the Son of God then He was a liar and a lunatic.

What about the doctrine of man? Some will say that man is basically good, but the Bible declares that "there is none righteous know not one all have sinned and come short of the glory of God" (Rom. 3:23).

These are some of the things that our churches haven't been teaching our new converts and as a matter of fact even older Christians perhaps mature or immature never hear these doctrines preached and taught form our pulpits. The reason I say this is that there are churches that are more concerned about programs, music, productions and just about everything else except for teaching and preaching the Word of God.

Now don't get me wrong. I don't think there's anything wrong with having programs, but when programs take the focus off of preaching God's Word and people getting saved then the programs have to go. Oh yeah I know some people are so in tune with the music that perhaps this is the only reason they come to church to start with. One church I went to was just like that. One lady in the church came for the music and when the preaching began she would get up and do her own thing. Now that's wrong. There's nothing wrong with having good music and I think good music is essential to our corporate worship, we are to sing praises to God and exalt Him with our singing, but once again some churches over emphasize the music portion of the service and that's wrong.

My brother in law is a fine pastor and preacher and is also a excellent musician. I say excellent because to me, anyone who can sing and play the guitar at the same time is good. Even though he likes music he was still focused on preaching the Word of God and that is important. One church I was in we sang for over 45 minutes. Sometimes we would sing the same song over and over and over where it becomes tiring and by the time the preacher is ready to preach we were ready to go home. In the same church we would sing for 45 minutes and the preacher would preach for 15 or 20 minutes and never invite people to come to Jesus. Whether we like it or not we have to make a biblical stance. We have a biblical mandate to grow in the grace and knowledge of our Lord Jesus Christ.

If all of our attention are focused upon these things then how is one to have the assurance of salvation and of course with that comes eternal security? That's the purpose for the writing of this book. The lay people who sit in our pews week after week might know about the doctrine of eternal security. They may call it by some other name such as once saved always saved, preservation of the saints or whatever name you give it, but they probably wouldn't be able to make a case for it.

I hope by the time you finish reading this book you see and understand my view on eternal security from a biblical standpoint, and not just my opinion. It doesn't really matter what my views are, if it isn't based upon the Word of God. This is an important doctrine and we must not take it lightly. At this point and time, if I could just put it in the simplest of terms, to fall away from grace would mean we would be eternally lost. I will expound on this in more depth later on.

Growing up with the Doctrine

When I was growing up we attended a Southern Baptist church which taught the doctrine of eternal security. That basically states that once you are saved, you are saved for all of eternity. I never understood it, nor did I question it. I just figured that was the way it was and that's it. I figured every denomination and every religious group of the world believed the same thing. Boy was I wrong.

I can remember walking the aisle to get saved as a young boy, not too young though, probably nine or 10. I have no doubt in my mind that the night I asked Jesus to come into my life He saved me. Although, as I got older I rebelled against God, the Church, and my parents. I was a rebellious child, but there isn't any doubt in my mind that in those rebellious days if I would have died I would have been in heaven. I don't believe for one minute that I had lost my salvation.

You might ask the question why would I believe such a thing? I believe it because I believe that the Bible teaches it. Salvation is a free gift. We certainly didn't do anything to earn it or deserve it and we cannot do anything to keep it or lose it. I hope and pray when all is said and done, that maybe just maybe the Holy Spirit might be able to convince those of you who are in doubt that the doctrine of eternal security is biblically based. Jesus himself taught that we are saved for all of eternity. Even though I was not living the Christian life I was still a child of God. When I was born into my family my mom and dad loved me. No matter what I did I was still a part of a family. My family! My parents were not going to throw me out of the family, no more than God would throw us out of his family for sinning. Let us look at a scripture or two so we can see this truth.

John 1:12 (KJV)

[12] But as many as received him, to them gave he power to become the sons of God, even to them that believe on his name:

So now He offers **Himself** to all **mankind** again and to those who **receive Him**, He gives the right or **authority to become children of God**. This verse tells us clearly how we can become children of God. It is not by good works, not by church membership, not by doing our best—but by **receiving Him, by believing in His Name.**

John 3:16 (KJV)

[16] For God so loved the world, that he gave his only begotten Son, that whosoever <u>believeth in him should not perish, but have everlasting life.</u>

This is perhaps one of the most quoted or misquoted verses in all the Bible. Many of us have memorized it as a child in Sunday school. I don't understand how we can take a verse of Scripture like this and add to it, as we do in so many ways. Take that word <u>everlasting (αἰώνιος, aiōnios) life</u>(ζωή, zōē) for example. Don't you think that if God didn't really mean everlasting life he would have used different words.

I think that it is interesting to look in the original language and get the right meaning and understanding of these words I don't want you to get the idea that I am a Greek scholar by any means for I am not but I like to dabble in the original language to get accurate meanings of the words.

ἀΐδιος, aidios Ahee-o'-nee-os

Usage Notes: denotes "everlasting" (from aei, "ever"), <u>Rom. 1:20</u>, RV, "everlasting," for AV, "eternal;" <u>Jude 1:6</u>, AV and RV "everlasting." Aiōnios, should always be translated "eternal" and aidios, "everlasting." "While aiōnios … negatives the end either of a space of time or of unmeasured time, and is used chiefly where something future is spoken of, aidios excludes interruption and lays stress upon permanence and unchangeableness" (Cremer). —Vine's Expository Dictionary of Old and New Testament Words

ζωή—zōē—**Usage Notes:** (Eng., "zoo," "zoology") is used in the NT "of life as a principle, life in the absolute sense, life as God has it, that which the Father has in Himself, and which He gave to the Incarnate Son to have in Himself, <u>John 5:26</u>, and which the Son manifested in the world, <u>1 John 1:2</u>. From this life man has become alienated in consequence of the fall, <u>Eph. 4:18</u>, and of this life men become partakers through faith in the Lord Jesus Christ, <u>John 3:15</u>, who becomes its Author to all such as trust in Him, <u>Acts 3:15</u>, and who is therefore said to be 'the life' of the believer, <u>Col. 3:4</u>, for the life that He gives He maintains, <u>John 6:35, 63</u>. Eternal life is the present actual possession of the believer because of his relationship with Christ, <u>John 5:24</u>; <u>1 John 3:14</u>, and that it will one day extend its domain to the sphere of the body is assured by the Resurrection of Christ, II Cor. 5:4; II Tim.1:10. This life is not merely a principle of power and mobility, however, for it has moral associations which are inseparable from it, as of holiness and righteousness. Death and sin, life and death and ejector of a holiness, are frequently contrasted in the Scriptures. —Vine's Expository Dictionary of Old and New Testament Words

Whether this verse was spoken by John or Jesus, it is God's Word and is an important summary of the gospel. God's motivation toward people is love. God's love is not limited to a few or to one group of people but His gift is for the whole world. God's love was expressed in the giving of His most priceless gift—His Son.

The Greek word translated one and only, referring to the Son, is μονογενής
Monogenēs which means "only begotten," or "only born-one." It is also used in John 1:14, 18; 3:18; and 1 John 4:9. On man's side, the gift is simply to be received, not earned (John 1:12-13). A person is saved by believing, by trusting in Christ. Perish (ἀπόλλυμι, apollymi) means not annihilation but rather a final destiny of "ruin" in hell apart from God who is life, truth, and joy. Eternal life is a new quality of life, which a believer has now as a present possession and will possess forever (cf. 10:28; 17:3). Walvoord, John F. ; Zuck, Roy B. ; Dallas Theological Seminary: The Bible Knowledge Commentary : An Exposition of the Scriptures. Wheaton, IL : Victor Books, 1983-c1985, S. 2:282

It doesn't make good sense to me that God would allow His only Son to die on the cross for just a few sins. I realize that God could do it anyway that He wanted to, but when He says that whosoever believe in Him speaking of His Son (Jesus Christ) has eternal life that is a promise from God the Father. The Bible says cannot lie.

Does eternal security give you a license to sin?

As promised earlier we are now going to talk about whether or not eternal security give us a license to sin, there are a lot of people who do not believe in or trust the doctrine of eternal security for this reason. They think maybe by some conceived notion that it gives us a license to sin. That is quite contrary to the Word of God. The apostle Paul in Romans chapter 5 talks about being reconciled to God and being justified by the blood of Jesus Christ. He will also talk about, in the same chapter, how sin came into the world by one man, but he also talks about the coming of a second man, Jesus, who reconciled us to God by his blood that was spilled upon Calvary Cross. Paul says that where sin abounds, Grace abounded much more. Then Paul continues on in the sixth chapter and makes a statement like this: "What shall we say then? Shall we continue in sin that grace may abound? God forbid". It means absolutely positively no.

I believe that the Bible speaks about two types of repentance first of all it speaks about repentance unto salvation.

Repentance unto salvation can only come by the drawing of the Holy Spirit. Once again the Bible is very clear. No one can be saved except the Spirit of God draw them and that is to convict them of their sins. When the Holy Spirit has convicted us of our sins then we have to ask Jesus Christ to forgive us of our sins and to cleanse us from all unrighteousness. If we really mean that with all sincerity, the Bible says that we will be saved. I don't believe there is any magic formula or a fancy prayer that needs to be prayed, but I do believe that there has to be the drawing of the Holy Spirit of God, and not our emotions or feelings.

It is true that there are a lot of people who walk the aisle on emotions or feelings and never experience the drawing of the Holy Spirit and therefore they walk away unfulfilled and perhaps not even saved. Once we are saved and we come to the other part of repentance .

I believe that every time we sin we lose the fellowship with God. I also believe that the more that we sin without repenting of those sins the easier it is to stay away from God. That's perhaps one of the reasons why people do not believe in eternal security.They see people who claim to be Christians but do not walk in faith.They walk in the way of the world.

It's easy to live in the world and be part of the world but Jesus told his disciples that we were to separate ourselves from the world and that means we are to live a godly life.

There are those people who never waver from the faith I have never been that person. Sometimes, even now, I am entertained by the idea of walking away from Christianity and denouncing the faith, but I don't believe that a real child of God could do that. Sure we get sidetracked sometimes. We get out of the will of God, sometimes we even backslide. One of the most important things in order to come back to God is true repentance. We have to ask God to forgive us of our sins and in His word as promised, He will do it. Sometimes we get busy in our lives and even in our days we forget to confess.

Some of my charismatic friends believe that the day they got saved was the day they quit sinning. Several years ago I encountered a pastor from the different denominational church, who said to me that it had been 25 years since he had sinned. When he got saved that was the day he quite sinning. I don't buy that for a minute. The day I quit sinning will be the day that I will either take my last breath on this earth, or will be the day when Jesus comes to get me. Either way we still sin after conversion.

I must say that we have to try, and it should be our desire not to sin, but as long as we are in this old clay shell we are sinners. We are not sinners because we sin, we sin because we are sinners. I don't know if that makes any sense, but because we are sinners that is our nature and that is our nature given to us by Adam. Therefore we sin because we are sinners but also on that same note we are sinless before the throne of God if we are a child of God because the blood of Jesus has covered us past, present, future sins they were all under the blood.

We have been reconciled to God and the Bible says that we have been justified to God that word justified actually means "just-as-if-I-have-never-sinned." We do get comfortable in our walk with Christ but never for a minute should we take our salvation lightly. We have to stay the course we have to finish the race and we must persevere to the end. Does eternal security give you a license to sin? God forbid.

I must say emphatically that the doctrine of eternal security in no way, shape, or form gives us a license to continue in sin. In fact the exact opposite is true. If we are truly born-again then it should be our desire not to sin. We should be striving to be like Christ, that is what keeps us from habitual sinning. We should sin less today than we did yesterday and sin less tomorrow than today.

If in fact if you believe that you can be saved and continue the same type of lifestyle chance's are you're not saved to start with. If you have the same kind of stinking thinking that you had before your so called conversion, then my friend you need some true repentance. True repentance is to agree with God that you are a sinner and to repent of those sins. It actually means making 180° turn, you have changed your mind about sin. The Bible also tells us that all have sinned and come short of the glory of God. That is the very first step we must take in order to know for certain that we are saved for all of eternity.

We were born in sin. We have lived our lives as sinful people. But when we come to Christ he imputes his righteousness in us. Coming to Christ is what makes all the difference in the world. If we are just playing church or going through the motions and there is no evidence of salvation in our lives because of the things that we are doing. Then I would recommend that you would have a self examination as Paul clearly tells us in I Corinthians. Because if there is no evidence of a changed life than my friend you're probably not saved to start with. To me that is where people get the wrong idea about eternal security. They think that every person who has ever professed Jesus Christ is saved, and that certainly is not the case. Coming to Christ requires true repentance.

Matt. 7:21-23

²¹ Not every one that saith unto me, Lord, Lord, shall enter into the kingdom of heaven; but he that doeth the will of my Father which is in heaven. ²² Many will say to me in that day, Lord, Lord, have we not prophesied in thy name? and in thy name have cast out devils? and in thy name done many wonderful works? ²³ And then will I profess unto them, I never knew you: depart from me, ye that work iniquity.

Scofield puts it this way:

"The Hebrew and Greek words for salvation imply the idea of deliverance, safety,preservation, healing, and soundness. Salvation is the great inclusive word of the Gospel, gathering into itself all the redemptive acts and processes: such as justification, redemption, grace, propitiation, imputation, forgiveness, sanctification, and glorification."

Salvation is in three tenses:

(1) The believer has been saved from the guilt and penalty of sin Luke 7:50; 1Cor1:18; 2Co 2:15; Eph 2:5, 8; 2Ti 1:9 is safe.

(2) The believer is being saved from the habit and dominion of sin Rom 6:14; Php 1:19; Php 2:12, 13; 2Th 2:13; Rom 8:2; Gal 2:19, 20; 2Co 3:18

(3) The believer is to be saved in the sense of entire conformity to Christ. Rom 13:11; Heb 10:36; 1Pe 1:5; 1Jn 3:2 Salvation is by grace through faith, is a free gift, and wholly without works Rom 3:27, 28; Rom 4:1-8; Rom 6:23; Eph 2:8

We did absolutely nothing to get salvation it wasn't up to us, and it certainly isn't up to us to keep it.

Romans 12: 1- **2**

[1] I beseech you therefore, brethren, by the mercies of God, that ye present your bodies a living sacrifice, holy, acceptable unto God, which is your reasonable service.

[2] And be not conformed to this world: but be ye transformed by the renewing of your mind, that ye may prove what is that good, and acceptable, and perfect, will of God.

Knowing Christ is a transformation from the inside out. If the Holy Spirit lives in us, would we not want to please God with our lives? Therefore if we truly are saved we will do all that we can to please God. We will not live our life the same way that we did before we were saved. How could we? We have a new nature, the nature of Christ living in us. So to get back to the original question does eternal security give me a license to sin. Absolutely positively not.

Romans 6:1-2 [1] What shall we say then? Shall we continue in sin, that grace may abound?

[2] God forbid. How shall we, that are dead to sin, live any longer therein?

According to this verse the apostle Paul tells us that God forbids that we continue in sin. And if we truly are born-again then we should not be doing the things or going to the places that we did before we got saved. Paul tells us again that we are a new creation.

II Cor. 5:17 Therefore if any man be in Christ, he is a new creature: old things are passed away; behold, all things are become new.

If we truly are a new creation in Christ, then we must have a new outlook on life. Being re-created in the image of our Lord Jesus Christ. We must therefore not be conformed to this world but as the Scripture says "be ye transformed by the renewing of your mind." Paul says that we are to have the mind of Christ. If Christ was sinless and He was then we should strive to be sinless. I know what you are thinking, how in the world can I be sinless in a world that is filled with sin? I never said that we would achieve that goal in this lifetime but it is something that we as the children of God should strive for. We will never be sinless in this world. That is the reason Christ had to come and die to start with. We are not sinners because we sin, we sin because we are sinners.

By the way, just how good do you have to be, or how much sin must you commit until you lose your salvation? What did Christ die for if you can earn your salvation and if you don't do enough good works to keep it or if you sin too much you will lose it? If that is the case then Christ died in vain and we who claim to be Christians will die in our sins. We can never be good enough to be righteous in the eyes of God not on our own merits. Remember the words of the apostle Paul in Romans chapter 7: 18.

[18] For I know that in me (that is, in my flesh,) dwelleth no good thing: for to will is present with me; but how to perform that which is good I find not.

So, how can we be eternally secure if the flesh is no good? Paul said "no good thing dwells in me". That means that we have no righteousness whatsoever. That means that we must agree with Isaiah when he says that our righteousness is like filthy rags in the eyes of God. That means once again that we are not saved on our own merits. If no good thing lives in me what would I have to base my salvation on?

Romans 3:10-12 (KJV)

[10] As it is written, There is none righteous, no, not one:

[11] There is none that understandeth, there is none that seeketh after God.

[12] They are all gone out of the way, they are together become unprofitable; there is none that doeth good, no, not one.

The Bible is pretty clear that we cannot earn our salvation. As a matter of fact the Bible tells us that we do not even try to seek after God on our own accords.

Before we are saved the old nature is this.The lust of the eyes, the lust of the flesh, and the pride of life. There is nothing spiritual about the flesh.

Chapter 8

Does Man have a free Will?

I would like for us to look at the doctrine of free will. The phrase "free will" is found in the Bible 16 times. All 16 times it means "voluntary." Fifteen of those times it's used of a free will (voluntary) offering. Not one of those 16 times does "free will" refer to salvation. Also, the idea that man has a "free will" independent from God's rule, probably had its origin in heathen, Greek philosophy.

Those Who Use the Phrase Free Will Rarely Define it
"Free will" is the topic everyone assumes, but few define. If "free will" is defined as the "ability and desire to will to receive Christ", it's then "free will." If it is defined as "voluntary to make choices",then humans have "free will."
We have free will in the sense we freely (voluntarily) will whatever we have both the desire and ability to do. God influences us by circumstances, thoughts, and power so we become voluntarily willing to fulfill His will. Perhaps a better phrase than "free will" is "voluntary will."
You may be surprised to discover that many Protestants share the Jesuit-Romanist view of free will. **Many Protestants Believe the Jesuit- Roman Catholic View of Free Will.**

The Roman Catholic Council of Trent, The Sixth Session: Justification)

Canon IV. If any one saith, that man's free will moved and excited by God, by assenting to God exciting and calling, no-wise **co-operates towards disposing and preparing itself for obtaining the grace of Justification;** that it cannot refuse its consent, if it would, but that, as something inanimate, it does nothing whatever and is merely passive; let him be anathema.

Canon V. If any one saith, that, since Adam's sin, the free will of man is lost and extinguished; or, that it is a thing with only a name, yea a name without a reality, a figment, in fine, introduced into the Church by Satan; let him be anathema.

I think that we all know, most people don't have the desire or the ability to come to Christ on their own. Once again they don't understand that since the fall, humans are spiritually dead, blind, and deaf, with no desire or ability to choose Christ. They don't see the need for God. They think that everything is just hunky-dory and when they've had enough of the good life then they will come to Christ. If that is the case then we could certainly wait until our deathbed to receive Christ.If our free will is enough then we wouldn't need the doctrines of predestination, election or perseverance of the saints. Is it our will or God's will that we are to be saved. That He predestinated us before the foundations of the world.

Did God predestine your adoption and inheritance according to your will, or His will?

"He chose us in Him before the foundation of the world... having predestinated us to adoption as sons by Jesus Christ to Himself, according to his good pleasure of His will" (Ephesians 1: 4-5)

"In Him also we have obtained an inheritance, being predestinated according to the purpose of Him who works all things according to the Council of His will" (Eph. 1:11)

Did God choose you because you would believe, or so that you would believe?

"God from the beginning choose you for salvation through sanctification by the Spirit and believe in the truth" (II Thess 2:13) Whose choice made the ultimate difference, the apostles' choice, or God's choice? **"You did not choose me, but I chose you** and appointed you that you should go and bear fruit" (Jn. 15:16)

Whose Will made Paul an apostle, his own will, or God's will?

"Paul, called to be an apostle of Jesus Christ through the will of God" (I Cor. 1: 1)
Did God call you according to your purpose (will,) or His purpose?
"And we know that all things work together for good to those who love God, to those who are called according to His purpose. For whom (not "what") He foreknew, He also predestined to be conformed to the image of His Son" (Rom. 8:28-29).
"Who has saved us and called us with a holy calling, not according to our works, but according to His own purpose and grace which was given to us in Christ Jesus before time began" (2 Tim. 1:9) According to the passages that we have just read, I believe that it is impossible for man to come to God on his own terms. Any gospel preaching that relies upon an act of the human will for the conversion of sinners has missed the mark.
Any sinner who supposes that his will has the strength to do any good accompanying salvation is greatly deluded and far from the kingdom. We are cast back upon the regenerating work of the Spirit of the living GOD. Unless GOD does something in the sinner, unless GOD creates a clean heart and renews a right

spirit within man, there is no hope of a saving change. While we address the wills of men in gospel preaching, their wills are bound in sin of an evil heart. But as we speak, and the LORD owns His word, sinners are quickened to life by divine power. His people are made willing in the day of His power (Psa 110:3). All who are adopted as sons of GOD were 'born not of the will of man, but of GOD.' (John1:13) We stand to preach with no power to make men change their will. Men cannot make themselves good, so no gimmicks or policies of men can persuade them to make the change but our glorious GOD, by inward, transforming power, can make a man repent. At this point we must say all glory be to GOD and to the Lamb! Salvation is of the LORD!

Chapter 9

The Two Views

In this chapter I would like to look at two different views concerning the topic of eternal security. I think we can safely say that there are two views concerning this precious doctrine and both views have scripture references to back them up. The views of which I speak of is Calvinism named for its leader John Calvin. Who is in favor of predestination, election, eternal security. The other view who is named after its leader also Jacob Arminius. Those that hold to this view can confidently say that their view is based on some 100 biblical passages. We of course will not look at all those in this book, but will point out a few. First I would like for us to see the view of Arminianism. There are five statements concerning this doctrine that I would like for us to see just to get an idea what separates these theologies.

The view of Arminianism
<u>Partial depravity</u>-This says in effect that man is a sinner, but not so bad that we cannot choose to come to God. It says that we are capable of choosing to accept salvation or not to choose salvation.

<u>Conditional election</u>-This simply says that God chose those who would be saved based on his foreknowledge of who would believe.

<u>Unlimited atonement</u>-This is perhaps the most accurate statement made by the Arminians. This says that Jesus died for everyone, even those who are not chosen and will not believe. Jesus death on the cross was for all humanity.

<u>Resistible grace</u>-This says that anyone who doesn't want to be saved doesn't have to be saved. This says that we can reject the call of God upon our lives. Basically the Arminians claim that the ultimate gift of salvation depends on our willingness to accept.

<u>Conditional salvation</u>-This says that a Christian who continues to live a life of sinning will fall away from God's grace.

About the only point that makes sense to me and that I believe is point number three. Unlimited atonement. I think the more we look through the Bible and see the teaching of Jesus we find that he died for an entire world.

I John 2:1-2

My little children, these things write I unto you, that ye sin not. And if any man sin, we have an advocate with the Father, Jesus Christ the righteous: ² And he is the propitiation for our sins: and not for ours only, but also for the sins of the whole world.

What an awesome verse, John tells his disciples those who are perhaps members of his church that we shouldn't sin, but if we do we have an advocate with the Father. That word "advocate" is a legal term referring to a litigator or someone that can plead our case before the Father. The word propitiation in verse number two carries with it the meaning of satisfaction. It means that Jesus Christ appeased God and was the satisfaction for our sins. The debt has been paid in full. Jesus' death on the cross was for an entire sinful world. This is not to say that the Arminians believe in a universal type salvation. In other words, they do not believe that everyone will be saved.

I don't believe in a universal salvation either because it is not biblical. To believe in a universal type salvation would mean to believe that everyone who ever lived or who will ever live will be saved and that my friend that is totally ridiculous. The Bible is very clear that there is only one way to heaven and that is Jesus. Now lets take a look at the other view called "Calvinism".

Calvinism

I hope that anyone who reads this book doesn't come away thinking that I am a five point Calvinist, which is the farthest thing from the truth. I do however think that John Calvin has some good points when it comes to salvation and keeping it. The following five categories do not comprise Calvinism in totality. They simply represent some of its main points.

Total Depravity

Since the fall of man we have been totally sinful.Everything that we are is without a doubt contributed by sin. We are completely sinful. We are completely affected by sin.

The doctrine of Total Depravity is derived from scriptures that reveal human character: Man's heart is evil (Mark 7:21-23) and sick (Jer. 17:9). Man is a slave of sin (Rom. 6:20). He does not seek for God (Rom. 3:10-12). He cannot understand spiritual things (1 Cor. 2:14). He is at enmity with God (Eph. 2:15),and is by nature a child of wrath (Eph. 2:3). The Calvinist asks the question, "In light of the scriptures that declare man's true nature as being utterly lost and incapable, how is it possible for anyone to choose or desire God?" The answer is, "He cannot. Therefore God must predestine."

Calvinism also maintains that because of our fallen nature we are born again not by our own will but God's will (John 1:12-13); God grants that we believe (Phil. 1:29); faith is the work of God (John 6:28-29); God appoints people to believe

(Acts 13:48); and God predestines (Eph. 1:1-11; Rom. 8:29; 9:9-23).

Unconditional Election

God does not base His election on anything He sees in the individual. He chooses the elect according to the kind intention of His will (Eph. 1:4-8; Rom. 9:11) without any consideration of merit within the individual.Nor does God look into the future to see who would pick Him. Also, as some are elected into salvation, others are not (Rom. 9:15, 21).

Limited Atonement

Jesus died only for the elect.Though Jesus' sacrifice was sufficient for all, it was not efficacious for all, meaning:(having the power to produce a desired effect). Jesus only bore the sins of the elect. Support for this position is drawn from such scriptures as Matt. 26:28 where Jesus died for 'many'; John 10:11, 15 which say that Jesus died for the sheep (not the goats, per Matt. 25:32-33); John 17:9 where Jesus in prayer interceded for the ones given Him, not those of the entire world; Acts 20:28 and Eph. 5:25-27 which state that the Church was purchased by Christ, not all people; and Isaiah 53:12 which is a prophecy of Jesus' crucifixion where he would bare the sins of many (not all).

Irresistible Grace

When God calls his elect into salvation, they cannot resist. God offers to all people the gospel message. This is called the external call. But to the elect, God extends an internal call and it cannot be resisted. This call is by the Holy Spirit who works in the hearts and minds of the elect to bring them to repentance and regeneration whereby they willingly and freely come to God. Some of the verses used in support this teaching are Romans 9:16 where it says that "it is not of him who wills nor of him who runs, but of God who has mercy"; Philippians 2:12-13 where God is said to be the one working salvation in the individual; John 6:28-29 where faith is declared to be the work of God; Acts 13:48 where God appoints people to believe; and John 1:12-13 where being born again is not by man's will, but by God's.

Perseverance of the Saints

You cannot lose your salvation.Because the Father has elected, the Son has redeemed, and the Holy Spirit has applied salvation, those thus saved are eternally secure. They are eternally secure in Christ. Some of the verses for this position are John 10:27-28 where Jesus said His sheep will never perish; John 6:47 where salvation is described as everlasting life; Romans 8:1 where it is said we have passed out of judgment; 1 Corinthians 10:13 where God promises to never let us be tempted beyond what we can handle; and Phil. 1:6 where God is the one being faithful to perfect us until the day of Jesus' return.

This of course is only a portion of these two views. I have a tendency to believe that John Calvin understood the theology of the election and predestination whereas Jacob Arminian might have been confused on the total depravity of man and our salvation. Arminianism says we will be saved on the conditions that we stay true to the Word of God and we don't have sin in our lives. If we do sin then our salvation is jeopardized. It just makes no sense to me whatsoever that a God who loves us so much would hinge that love on whether or not we could be good enough. Once again I have to say that the Bible is clear. If we are truly the sons and daughters of God- that is to say if we truly have a personal relationship with Jesus Christ our Lord and Savior- I believe that we can say with all assurance the words that Fanny Crosby penned so long ago.

Blessed assurance Jesus is mine ! Oh what a foretaste of glory Divine! Heir of salvation purchase of God, born of his spirit washed in his blood.

This is my story this is my song, praising of my Savior all the day long; this is my story this is my song, praising my Savior all the day long. (The Baptist Hymnal p334 Fanny Crosby).

Yet you may still be unconvinced by these two views, of this most important doctrine. If you'll take a look at these scripture references that I have just given you then perhaps you'll have a better understanding. I don't want to be an encourager of Calvinism or Arminianism. Someone told me long ago that you were either a Calvinist or a Arminian I don't necessarily agree with that either. I do believe that we can search the Scriptures for ourselves and make this conclusion on our own. Let me just say that it's not something that we should take lightly but with much prayer and meditation searching the Scriptures to find the truth. I think that one of the saddest things that can be said as a Christian is that we don't have any assurance of our salvation. Eternal security and assurance are two different issues. Perhaps this might be a fitting time to look at our assurance of salvation.

Chapter 10

The Doctrine of Assurance

This reminds me of the children's song "If you're saved and you know it clap your hands." I think perhaps some people cannot sing that song with all assurance. Salvation is not an "I hope so, I think so salvation". John said "I have written these things that you might know that you have eternal life".

I John 5:13 These things have I written unto you that believe on the name of the Son of God; that ye may know that ye have eternal life, and that ye may believe on the name of the Son of God.

II Cor.13:5 Examine yourselves, whether ye be in the faith; prove your own selves. Know ye not your own selves, how that Jesus Christ is in you, except ye be reprobates?

I understand that this doctrine of assurance of salvation can be most complicated as well. Sometimes I don't feel much like a Christian sometimes I don't even act like a Christian but I have the assurance that I am a Christian. How do I know that I am a Christian you ask? Let me give you my testimony briefly. One of my life passages in the Bible is I Corinthians 6: 9-12. Before I came to know the Lord Jesus Christ as my personal savior I was nothing more or less than a drunk. Although I did grow up in a Christian home and made a profession of faith at the age of nine, I was still a drunk. As I said in a previous chapter I was a rebellious child and I rebelled against God even though I had asked Jesus to save me. That's why these verses are so important to me.

[9] Know ye not that the unrighteous shall not inherit the kingdom of God? Be not deceived: neither fornicators, nor idolaters, nor adulterers, nor effeminate, nor abusers of themselves with mankind, [10] Nor thieves, nor covetous, nor drunkards, nor revilers, nor extortioners, shall inherit the kingdom of God. [11] And such were some of you: but ye are washed, but ye are sanctified, but ye are justified in the name of the Lord Jesus, and by the Spirit of our God.

The scripture says that the unrighteous shall not inherit the kingdom of God. We are unrighteous in the eyes of God, until we allow the blood of Jesus to cleanse us from all unrighteousness. I believe that many of us can place ourselves into these categories that are mentioned above. Even if we have just one sin accredited to our account we are still unrighteous in the eyes of God. My life was going nowhere fast my marriage was about to end. I was 27 years old and had two children who my wife raised for the first five years of their lives because I was too busy closing up the bars. I'm not proud of that testimony by any means but as we can clearly see, men are totally depraved. No matter what background you come from we are all sinners who have been saved by the grace of God. Even back in my rebellious days the Holy Spirit was still working on me. It took an act of repentance on my part to allow the Spirit of God to work in me. I know that I have been saved because of the change that Jesus made in my life, I no longer do the same things that I did before I was saved, I now have a new desires a real hunger and thirst for righteousness. The transformation was made from the inside out. When we ask Christ to come into our lives and are serious about it then we are saved.

The Bible says whosoever shall call upon the name of the Lord shall be saved. It never says anything about being saved for a short period of time or until we sin again. Assurance is to have the confidence in knowing that when you asked Jesus to save you, He did just that. When He saves us it is for all of eternity. He gave you eternal life.

Eternal security is biblically true whether we have the assurance of our salvation or not. Perhaps this is the reason why a lot of people have the I hope so salvation when it comes to heaven because you lack the assurance.

Sometimes the lack of assurance is due to sin creeping back into our lives. We have doubts of our conversion experience because we do not have the assurance of being kept saved. You may ask the question how can I be assured that I am saved? The answer to that question is very simple have you done exactly what the Bible tells us to do in order to obtain salvation. Whosoever shall call upon the name of the Lord shall be saved. No ifs ands or buts about it.

If you are sick and tired of your sin and it looks like there's no way out and you ask Jesus to forgive you of your sins, He will do it. The proof my friend is in the pudding. You desire Jesus more than the world and you love the brethren. John says that if we say we love God and hate our brothers that we are a liar and the truth is not in us. He who loves the brethren also loves God. (My paraphrase)

Jesus said if you love me keep my commandmentsI am the vine, ye are the branches: He that abideth in me, and I in him, the same bringeth forth much fruit: for without me ye can do nothing.

If we are producing fruits as Christians that means that we are indeed abiding in the vine which is Jesus. If we are abiding in Jesus and He in us then the proof is in our outward appearance for we can do nothing without Christ. If we could just take God at his Word and believe Him then we would have all the assurance that we need. Look at these two scripture references.

John 5:24 Verily, verily, I say unto you, He that heareth my word, and believeth on him that sent me, hath everlasting life, and shall not come into condemnation; but is passed from death unto life.

I John 5:1 Whosoever believeth that Jesus is the Christ is born of God: and every one that loveth him that begat loveth him also that is begotten of him.

These things have I written unto you that believe on the name of the Son of God; that ye may know that ye have eternal life, and that ye may believe on the name of the Son of God.

Dr. Robert Gromacki has in his book, Salvation is Forever, pp 177-182 a list of 12 things that we can test of our salvation experience.

1. Have you enjoyed spiritual fellowship with God, with Christ, and with fellow believers? (I John 1: 3, 4)
2. Do you have a sensitivity to sin? (I John 1:5-10)
3. Are you basically obedient to the commandments of scripture? (I John 2:3-5)
4. What is your attitude toward the world and its values? (I John 2:15)
5. Do you love Jesus Christ and look forward to His coming? (II Timothy 4:8; I John 3: 2,3)
6. Do you practice sin less now that you have professed faith in Christ? (I John 3:5, 6)
7. Do you love other believers? (I John 3: 14)
8. Have you experienced answered prayers? (I John 3: 22; 5: 14, 15)
9. Do you have the inner witness of the Holy Spirit? (Romans 8: 15; I John 4: 13)
10. Do you have the ability to discern between spiritual truth and error? (John 10: 3-5, 27; I John 4: 1-6)
11. Do you believe the basic doctrines of the faith? (I John 5: 1)
12. Have you experienced persecution for your Christian position? (John 15:18-20; Philippians 1: 28)

(Salvation is Forever, pp. 177-182)

Let's just take God at his word and see where He will lead us.

Chapter 11

The Unpardonable Sin

A lot of people think that they can commit the unpardonable sin. I won't spend a great deal of time on this subject but I will say that I must agree with the scholars who say that it is impossible to commit the sin today. I have had people come and ask me pastor is it possible that I could commit the unpardonable sin. Of course I say no it isn't but I would like to give a brief explanation of what I mean. Did you know that there are hundreds of verses in the Bible that promise the forgiveness of sins. Whatever I think about the unpardonable sin I can only find one scripture reference to it. (Matthew 12:31-32)

[31] Wherefore I say unto you, All manner of sin and blasphemy shall be forgiven unto men: but the blasphemy against the Holy Ghost shall not be forgiven unto men. [32] And whosoever speaketh a word against the Son of man, it shall be forgiven him: but whosoever speaketh against the Holy Ghost, it shall not be forgiven him, neither in this world,

What is the reason for this harshness that Jesus speaks about not forgiving those who speak against the Holy Ghost. Jesus says that all manner of sin and blasphemy shall be forgiven but the blasphemy of the Holy Ghost shall not be forgiven of the man. This passage is a direct reference to the Pharisees who had witnessed the undeniable power that our Lord Jesus Christ was performing miracles in the power of the Holy Spirit. Yet the Pharisees plotted against Jesus and blasphemed Him and accusing Him that his power came from Satanic forces. The Pharisees were witnesses to all that Jesus did and spake, yet they denied Him and denied His deity.Because the Pharisees did not recognize Jesus as God openly, they were willing to go to the devils hell.You can't help but to wonder if they truly did believe that Jesus was God,but wanted to go with the crowd.I don't believe that the unpardonable sin is for us today for the simple fact that Jesus died for <u>all</u> of our sins <u>every single one</u>. Make no mistake about it though, there is a sin that will never be pardoned. Well wait a minute.You just said that there is no unpardonable sin. That's right I did say that. But what I am talking about is when you take that last breath of life and you go out into eternity without Jesus Christ you will never be pardoned for that. Where you spend eternity is determined here and now, not after we die. Think about this for a minute. You spend eternity separated from the love of God. How sad is that? If you believe that you have committed the unpardonable sin, let me assure you that you have not. The Bible is full of passages that tell of God's love and forgiveness no matter what our circumstances are. There is no sin that God can't or will not forgive.

Chapter 12

Falling from Grace

Help me! I have fallen and I can't get up! Remembered that television commercial? Sometimes I think that we feel like that old woman on the television commercial who had fallen and couldn't get up. Sometimes we slip and fall in our Christian walk. What I mean by that is that we may fall in the sin trap of life but I can tell you with all assurance that we haven't fallen from grace.

Let's examine the facts and see exactly what it means to fall from grace. In a church that I had pastored previously a young man came up to me and said "pastor I think I have fallen from grace" this was of course a shock to hear someone say that, so I asked the young man, "Why do believe you have fallen from grace"? His response was "I don't have the zeal for Christ as I once did. I don't have the desire to serve like I once did." One of the reasons he didn't have the zeal that he once had for Christ was the fact that sin was creeping back into his life. He was a fairly new Christian and didn't understand the passage that he had read about falling from grace. He figured that as long as he was still sinning and that he had lost his passion for Christianity then he thought that God had lost His passion for him. It is safe in saying that if this phrase "falling from grace" can be associated with loosing our salvation this could all stem from not having full assurance of our salvation. It wasn't until I fully examine the facts about this passage that I was able to correct his theology on this passage. So let me show you exactly what this passage means and who is directed to.

Gal. 5:1-5 Stand fast therefore in the liberty wherewith Christ hath made us free, and be not entangled again with the yoke of bondage. [2] Behold, I Paul say unto you, that if ye be circumcised, Christ shall profit you nothing. [3] For I testify again to every man that is circumcised, that he is a debtor to do the whole law. [4] Christ is become of no effect unto you, whosoever of you are justified by the law; ye are fallen from grace. [5] For we through the Spirit wait for the hope of righteousness by faith.

This is a great passage in the book of Galatians. Now Paul was talking to the church at Galatia. At this time in Galatia there was a group of false teachers called the Judaizers. These Judaizers taught a gospel that was a similar to what Paul taught but they wanted to add to the gift of salvation. They wanted the Christians to place their faith in Christ but to add to it by keeping portions of the law. One of the most important parts of their gospel was that they needed to be circumcised. And if you can imagine that these Judaizers persuaded some of the Gentiles to do just that.

The Gentiles of course looked at it a different way, they wanted to make sure beyond any shadow of a doubt that they were saved. If that ment not only placing their faith in Christ only, but also adding the act of circumcision to their faith then that's what they would do. Look what it says in verse two; Paul says that if you are circumcised, then Christ shall profit you nothing.

What in fact that really says is that if you feel the need to be circumcised or even in our day and age to add something to it such as baptism or church membership or anything of the like then Christ death on the cross would be _nullified_ .In other words, it wouldn't mean a thing. As a pastor who believes that in teaching our parishioners the truth from God's Word, it is heartbreaking when you think that your people are strong in Biblical doctrines and then something like this adding to our salvation comes up it breaks our heart, just to know that people do not place their faith in Jesus and Jesus alone.

If I feel that way about the people I teach, think how the apostle Paul must have thought about the church at Galatia. There is no possible way to know everything that the Judaizers taught but one thing we know for sure is that they believed in salvation by works. Much like some of the denominations that we have today.

Not only did they believe in salvation by works, they also believed in keeping the mosaic law or at least portions of it. Circumcision was part of keeping the law, not only placing their faith in Christ but adding to that faith circumcision, then that's what they would do. So by now you're probably asking the question what does this have to do with falling from grace?

Well once again let's examine the facts. Paul says that we are to stand fast in the liberty wherein Christ hath made us free. I think the major concern of Paul was that, the Galatians were going back into bondage, drifting away from the freedom that only Christ can give. The Judaizers was placing stipulations on their salvation. The Gentiles were about to enter a religion that was going to restrict their freedom in Christ. They were about to fall for a religion that was going to force them to work in order to keep their salvation.

Galatians 5:3-4 (NASB77)

3 And I testify again to every man who receives circumcision, that he is under obligation to keep the whole Law. 4 You have been severed from Christ, you who are seeking to be justified by law; you have fallen from grace.

Paul is very stern in his rebuke to the Gentiles. He says that if you believe that you can be justified by the law, then you're severed from Christ. Nowhere in the Bible does it say that we are justified by the law and Paul was trying to make a clear statement saying that if the law would justify us from our sins then Christ's death on the cross is nullified. It means nothing absolutely nothing.

Paul says in verse three *"for I testify again to every man that is circumcised that he is a debtor to the law"*. Paul was in effect saying that if you choose to add to your salvation the works of the law that you had better keep the whole law. You cannot pick and choose which laws you are going to keep. Then he goes on in verse number four to say *"Christ is become of no effect unto you whosoever of you are justified by the law; ye are fallen from grace"*.

This word *"no effect"* is better rendered <u>severed </u>from Christ. The whole point that Paul is trying to make to the Gentiles is this- if the Judaizers doctrines are the correct doctrines then Christ dying on the cross was unnecessary. Paul wasn't telling the Gentiles that they were in danger of losing their salvation but in fact they were in danger of losing their freedom in Christ. <u>He never mentions in these verses that you have fallen from salvation.</u> The Bible says that we are saved by grace not of works. Paul's biggest concern for the church at Galatia was that they were going to place themselves in bondage of the law and abandoned the grace of God. There may be people out there today that feel as though they have fallen from grace and in a sense they may just do that by adding works to salvation. But let me make this as crystal clear as I possibly can: the apostle Paul says that you will never, ever under any circumstance lose or fall from <u>salvation.</u>

What if I fall away?

Heb. 6:4-6 **For it** is <u>impossible</u> for those who were <u>once enlightened,</u> and have <u>tasted of the heavenly gift,</u> and were made partakers of the Holy Ghost, [5] And have tasted the good word of God, and the powers of the world to come, [6] If they shall fall away, to renew them again unto repentance; seeing they crucify to themselves the Son of God afresh, and put him to an open shame.

It goes without saying that this passage of Scripture is perhaps one of the most if not the most controversial passage in the entire Bible as far as salvation is concerned. Several commentators have bypassed this passage in there commentaries. Others have skimmed over it lightly and then there are those who have given a complete commentary on the subject.

There are those that will say "see I knew it all along I can lose my salvation". Let me say wait a minute before you draw your conclusions on this verse. There are different viewpoints on this passage of Scripture which I would like for us to examine to find out which best fits in this passage. Perhaps the most unsatisfactory explanation of these scriptures are the ones that say that these Christians have lost their salvation.

There are many people who hold this view. Even some of the most prominent Christians adhere to this view. I must say I am not comfortable at all with this view, knowing that if I were able to lose my salvation to be re-saved (if I could use the phrase) would be impossible.

There are a lot of people today who because of the position that they take on this passage do not enjoy their salvation nor could they enjoy it, not knowing if they were going to lose it.

There is another view that has some merit to it and that is that some people say that this is a "hypothetical case". Which of course sounds pretty reasonable and if I didn't favor a different interpretation of this passage then this would probably be the one that I would accept. Here is another interpretation of this passage. That in <u>verse 6</u>, there really is no "if" in the Greek. It is a participle and should be translated "having fallen away." Therefore these folk have another interpretation, which is that the passage speaks of mere professors, not genuine believers. They only profess to be Christians. This is the view which I adhere as do such scholars as Matthew Henry, F. W. Grant, and J. N. Darby, as does C. I. Scofield in his excellent reference Bible. Let me show you why I like this interpretation.

If you will notice with me this passage makes no reference to salvation. Once again there is no mention of justification, sanctification, glorification, or regeneration. Looking at this passage carefully I think that we can determine that this passage is not talking to those who have been born again. The very first thing that I want you to see is the phrase "it is impossible" ἀδύνατος, *adynatos*. Obviously this means exactly what it says. It is impossible for those who have been enlightened. Some commentators have gone as far out on a limb to say that it could be achieved with high difficulty. Where these guys come up with this stuff I have no idea. But make no bones about it, the <u>Bible says that it is impossible for those who have been enlightened</u>. The message that I want to convey here is there is no possibility, not that it was somewhat difficult but it is impossible.

It speaks to those who have been enlightened. I would like for us to examine this word enlightened. You may be saying to yourself right now if I have been enlightened by the Gospel doesn't it mean that somewhere in the past I have received Christ as Savior? Not necessarily because there are those out there who have seen and tasted of the Gospel or the Word of God but have simply never professed Christ as Lord. Just because one has a head knowledge of Christ and the Gospel does not mean that he has been transformed into the image of Christ. If you notice with me this word enlightened is the Greek word (*phōtizō*). Several times it is translated "to give light by knowledge or teaching." What this basically says is that you can learn about something and have that knowledge or have been taught about it but not really experienced it. Let me give you an example of knowing something but not really experiencing it. When I was a young man I went to a community college in order to acquire a trade I took courses in air conditioning and heating and I thought that when I graduated I knew everything there was to know about the heating and air conditioning business. Boy was I wrong. I remember getting out on my first job. It was actually rewiring a furnace for my dad that should have taken about 20 minutes but instead it took me half a day and I burnt up two transformers in the process. You see I had book knowledge but I never had practical experience. Even though these Hebrews had the Gospel preached to them and some of them may have seen Jesus, heard his teachings saw his miracles and had intellect of who he was or what he was capable of doing, but they just did not believe that he was the Son of God, the Messiah, and therefore went back to Judaism.

Even this portion of Scripture I just don't understand, especially when you relize that first century Jews or Christians had the opportunity to be with Jesus, to walk with Him and to talk with Him and probably watched His every move yet came away as an unbeliever.

Perhaps even in our own churches this goes on today as the Gospel is preached, peoples hearts are softened to a place of repentance but they never take that step of faith and acknowledge Jesus as the savior of the world, the one and only one that can forgive our sins. Some of them come so close to salvation but never accept Christ.

Therefore they have exhausted perhaps their last opportunity to be saved. When a person crosses that threshold they will drift off into eternity separated from the love of God and go to a devils hell.

Not only had they see the heavenly light but had also tasted of the heavenly gift. You might ask yourself what exactly is the heavenly gift. It could be referring to a couple of different things like the Holy Spirit but seeing how the Holy Spirit is specifically mentioned in the next verse I see this as referring to Jesus himself. As we look upon this verse we can see that the heavenly gift was not eaten but only tasted. What do I mean by that? The gift of salvation was not actually received, it was only examined to see if it would fit their lifestyle. Not only does this verse speak of Jesus as being the heavenly gift, but also of what Jesus brings, the gift of salvation.

This is very important because we have people in our churches all the time who are on the brink of salvation but never come to accept Christ as Lord and Savior. They have tasted of the heavenly gift but they have never received the gift. There is a big difference between church membership and a personal relationship with Jesus.

This is perhaps what this verse implies, the people that the writer of Hebrews was talking about have been enlightened with the word they have seen the heavenly gift, they have tasted of that gift but never ever received it. Most of the time when I taste of something that I like, it just whets my appetite for more and when I get a taste of something that isn't too appealing then I have to spit it out. The Bible says that they tasted of the heavenly gift but were not partakers of it. It is above my comprehension how people can stay in church week after week and hear the word of God preached and to taste of the Word of God yet never give their lives to Christ.

Let's move on to the next part of the verse where it says they are partakers of the Holy Ghost. The Greek word (*metochos*) has to do with association, not possession. I think it is safe to say that these Jews had been around Jesus and the Word of God and yet they did not possess the Holy Spirit they were never saved.

Whenever the Bible speaks about Christians and the Holy Spirit it always refers to the Christian being filled with the Spirit and also the spirit indwelling the believer. It never speaks of a Christian or a believer being associated with the Holy Spirit.

Let us move to the next part of this verse. It is plain to see that once again these Jews are referred to as tasting something from God. This time he refers to the Word of God. This is an interesting word but is not the same word that is used in John 1:1 where it talks about in the beginning was the Word. That word is λόγος, *logos.* This is a title of Jesus and it refers to the Word of life. However, the word used in this verse is the word ρήμα, *rhēma* denotes "that which is spoken, what is uttered in speech or writing;" in the singular, "a word,"—Vine's Expository Dictionary of Old and New Testament Words.

These two words are different.The fact that *Logos* means the entire Word of God or the living Word of God. As for the word *Rhema* it denotes a portion of the Word of God which is very fitting in this case. It fits very well here because they have tasted of the heavenly gift, they saw and heard the Gospel yet they rejected the Word of God.

Tasting is perhaps the first step towards salvation. *Faith cometh by hearing and hearing by the word of God.* Sometimes people dabble in Christianity just as they do in anything else without really coming to a saving knowledge and entering a relationship with Jesus Christ. I believe that is what this passage is talking about - professors but not heart possessors.

Chapter 13

What about Apostasy?

Can a person really turn their back on the Lord Jesus Christ? Can you really deny that you know Him? What does apostasy mean?

1 : renunciation of a religious faith **2** : abandonment of a previous loyalty : defection

New Testament The English word "apostasy" is derived from a Greek word (*apostasia*) that means, "to stand away from." The Greek noun occurs twice in the New Testament (Acts 21:21; 2 Thess. 2:3), though it is not translated as "apostasy" in the King James Version. A related noun is used for a divorce (Matt. 5:31; 19:7; Mark 10:4). The corresponding Greek verb occurs nine times   *Holman Bible Dictionary*

The Bible does teach apostasy, but it is important for us to know what this means.

Apostasy does not refer to true believers who have eternal life and then fall away, which is a contradiction in terms. Instead, it refers to professing believers who showed that they never truly believed by later renouncing the faith. The apostle John explains in.

1 John 2:19 (KJV)

[19] They went out from us, but they were not of us; for if they had been of us, they would no doubt have continued with us:

but they went out, that they might be made manifest that they were not all of us.

I don't believe that a child of God is going to renounce his or her salvation. If we are truly saved it is impossible for a person to turn their back on the Lord Jesus Christ. Sometimes we may step out of His will and even backslide for some time, but that doesn't mean that we have renounced our salvation. If for some unforeseen reason you could, I can't understand why a person would do that. Having a relationship with Jesus is our only hope. Jesus is our comfort in time of distress, He is our rest when we are weary. He is our strength in time of weakness, He loves us when we are unloving. No matter what our circumstance, Jesus is always going to be there to see us through. The bible says that He is closer than a brother the bible says He is the same yesterday, today, and tomorrow. He never changes.

Several years ago a good friend of mine confided in me that he was a born again Christian but quit serving God after the death of a child. Our conversation focused on what caused this turnaround to quit serving God. He assured me that there was a time in his life that he asked the Lord Jesus Christ to save him and he says I know beyond any shadow of a doubt that I was saved. He also shared with me this verse stating that since he renounced Jesus Christ as Lord and Savior that he would be lost for eternity.

That statement bothered me immensely. I could not get that out of my mind for the life of me so I decided to do some research on this passage. I have come to draw the conclusion that if a person is truly saved then they cannot lose their salvation or give it back. Now as for my friend I can't know for certain if he was indeed saved. I can only take his word for it, but there simply is no evidence that he is or ever was saved.

I this passage teaches that those who have turned her back on Christ (apostasy) were not truly saved to start with. By dissecting this verse word by word we can see that if a person was able to lose their salvation or even to give it up then it would be utterly impossible for them to renew their salvation.

What a sad commentary that would be for God the Creator of the entire universe. He loves us so much that He gave his only begotten Son that whosoever believes in Him <u>should not perish but have everlasting life</u>. If God promises that to those that believe on His dear Son, then how could we diminish the love and the grace of God by saying that we don't love God anymore and we are not going to serve Him anymore and give our salvation back to Him?

Salvation my friend is a free gift, and God is not going to take it back, not even if we sin and not even if we to denounce Jesus Christ. There is nothing that is able to separate us from God's love. I believe the Scriptures speak for themselves. He preordained us to be saved from eternity past to eternity future.

Whenever we think of apostasy we must look at the book of Jude. Without getting into great detail about apostasy I would like to ever so briefly touch on it, skim over the top if you would.

Don't you just love his first verse in Jude?

Jude 1:1 (KJV)

[1] Jude, the servant of Jesus Christ, and brother of James, to them that are sanctified by God the Father, and preserved in Jesus Christ, and called:

Jude in his little but mighty book written to Christians warns about the day of apostasy. The bible says that we who are Christians are preserved in Christ Jesus. Now what exactly does that mean "preserved in Christ Jesus"? It means to be kept; to be preserved; to care; to keep in custody; to be guarded and watched after. Believers are "preserved in Jesus Christ." God keeps the believer, guards and watches over him. —Practical Word Studies in the New Testament

"And called." Not only are we preserved in Jesus Christ, safe in Him, but we are also called. The word called, as it is used in Scripture, is not only an invitation that is sent out, but it is an invitation that is sent out and accepted and made real because of the Spirit of God."—J. Vernon McGee's Thru The Bible

The falling away is real, and is a real threat to Christianity because there are so many people who profess with their mouth but do not possess in their hearts the Lord Jesus, there will come a day when those who profess with their mouth they will find out just how wrong they really were. Don't allow yourself to be in that group of people you can know for sure that you have eternal life. There is a difference in knowing about Jesus and having a personal relationship with Him.

If you would do a complete study in the book of Jude you would soon realize that apostasy started with the fall of man and has come full circle in our churches today as it did in the day of Jesus and even when Jude wrote his epistle. It is my prayer that we would pray for those who seem to be in the state of apostasy, that the gospel would prick their hearts and that they would repent.

Conclusion

Well it is my prayer that after reading this book you have concluded that eternal security is real. It is something that we can experience here and now, just knowing that when we have taken that last breath of life we will be ushered into the gates of splendor.

Knowing that we have been born again it should be our hearts desire to do everything that we possibly can to please God. That's why these doctrines are so important to our walk with Christ. We should take these doctrines to heart and learn to appreciate all that God has done for us. He has adopted us into His family, He has given us the assurance of our salvation, He has pardoned us from our iniquitics. God has sccured us in Ilis Son. Praise God, praise God, praise God.

Index

Merriam-Webster, Inc: *Merriam-Webster's Collegiate Dictionary*. 10th ed. Springfield, Mass., U.S.A. : Merriam-Webster, 1996, c1993

Quote from Adrian-isms the wit and wisdom of Adrian Rogers page 172

(Holman Bible dictionary)

Holman Bible Dictionary

Shorter Catechism, Question 34

Dr. C.I. Schofield

Southern Baptist Convention Baptist Faith and Message

Covington Theological Seminary Dr. James Hutchings

Masters Graduate School of Divinity Dr. Dennis Fry

Vine's Expository Dictionary of Old and New Testament Words

Walvoord, John F. ; Zuck, Roy B. ; Dallas Theological Seminary: *The Bible Knowledge Commentary : An Exposition of the Scriptures*. Wheaton, IL : Victor Books, 1983-c1985, S. 2:282

The Baptist Hymnal p334 Fanny Crosby).

Dr. Robert Gromacki in his book salvation is forever pp 177-182 is a list of 12 things that we can test of our salvation experience.

Practical Word Studies in the New Testament

J. Vernon McGee's Thru The Bible